MASTERING
CLINICAL
RESEARCH

Pathway to a Six-Figure Career

NADINE H. SPRING, PhD

ISBN: 978-1-968061-34-0

Welcome to Your Six-Figure Career Pathway

If you've picked up this book, chances are you're looking for more—from your career, your income, and your impact.

Maybe you're already in healthcare and feeling burnt out.

Maybe you're curious about clinical research but don't know where to start.

Or maybe you've heard about six-figure roles in the industry and thought: *"That could be me... if someone just showed me how."*

This book is your HOW.

Mastering Clinical Research: Pathway to a Six-Figure Career was created for people just like you—ambitious, skilled, and ready for a clear, step-by-step roadmap into a rewarding field that's growing fast and hungry for talent.

What You'll Learn:

In the pages ahead, you'll discover:

- What clinical research is and why it's one of the best-kept secrets in healthcare careers
- The different roles available (like Clinical Research Coordinator and CRA), and what it takes to land them
- How to write a standout resume—even if you have no direct experience
- Interview strategies that get you hired

- And how to grow into six-figure roles without needing another degree

This isn't theory. This is practical, actionable, real-world guidance based on years of industry experience, coaching, and mentoring.

Whether you are a nurse, medical assistant, lab tech, public health grad, or simply someone looking for a meaningful, upward-moving career—this book will show you how to step confidently into clinical research and start building your six-figure future.

So grab a highlighter, take notes, and most of all—believe this:

The clinical research industry is waiting for you. And your journey starts right now.

Let's dive in.

Nadine Spring, PhD

Table of Contents

Acknowledgements

I am deeply grateful to all those who have contributed to the creation of this book, *Mastering Clinical Research: Pathway to a Six-Figure Career*.

Firstly, I extend my heartfelt thanks to my mentors who have guided me throughout my career. Your wisdom, encouragement, and unwavering support have been invaluable in shaping my professional journey and in the development of this book. Your insights and advice have not only helped me navigate the complexities of clinical research but have also inspired me to share my knowledge with others aspiring to excel in this field.

I would also like to acknowledge the countless patient volunteers whose participation in clinical trials often goes unrecognized. Their willingness to contribute to research is a testament to their courage and altruism. These unsung heroes are integral to advancing medical knowledge and improving patient care, and their contributions are deeply appreciated.

To my son, Logan, your patience and understanding have been a constant source of strength. Your support, despite the many hours spent in my home office while working on the book, has been a reminder of what truly matters and has fueled my dedication to this project. Your motivation to remind me to work and write is always the cutest!

Thank you all for your roles in this journey and for making this endeavor possible.

Lots of Love,
xoxo,
Nadine

My Personal Journey to Clinical Research

From an early age, I was captivated by the worlds of math and science. Numbers and formulas made sense to me in a way that almost always felt intuitive, and I excelled in these subjects throughout my schooling. I often represented my school in math competitions, enjoying the challenge of problem-solving and logical thinking. This passion led me to become the first in my family to obtain a bachelor's degree. Those years were filled with both excitement and uncertainty. I had a love for science and a desire to make an impact, and I ultimately chose biology as my major, setting out on what I thought would be a clear-cut path toward a career in medicine. One of the things I loved about studying biology was all the math factored into the chemistry, physics, and calculus courses.

When I began my undergrad journey, I didn't recall hearing terms such as "public health" or "health equity." My singular focus was to become a physician, a neurosurgeon in particular. That's what my parents told me I needed to do. Yet, as I progressed through my undergraduate studies, I found myself questioning whether that was truly the right path for me. The idea of a Ph.D. started to pique my interest because I also knew that I wasn't drawn to the aspects of medicine that required dealing with bodily fluids. I didn't want to directly get in contact with germs. I wanted to help people, and as I explored career pathways more, I soon realized that direct patient care wasn't the only way to do that.

After earning my bachelor's degree in biology, I took my first steps into the world of research through an entry-level position at Mount Sinai Medical Center, working under Dr. Michelle Gong. My first job was as a research assistant. It was there that I was first introduced to clinical research, a field I had never previously considered. In fact, I didn't realize this world of careers existed in high school. I quickly became fascinated by the process and how scientific rigor and data-driven decision-making could shape the future of medicine. While working at Mount Sinai, I also discovered their Master of Public Health (MPH) program, which led me to enroll in courses and, ultimately, fall in love with public health.

As I deepened my understanding of research, my career continued to evolve. I became a Research Coordinator, then Lupus Center Research Manager at the Hospital for Special Surgery. This was a defining moment in my career. I saw firsthand how clinical trials could transform the lives of individuals living with chronic conditions, many of whom had few or no treatment options for their conditions. It was in this role that I realized we needed to do more to advance care for underrepresented populations. I, myself, am underrepresented in medicine. People needed to be aware that clinical trials were not just experimental studies but an opportunity for access to cutting-edge therapies that could change lives.

With a growing passion for research and advocacy, I ended up pursuing a master's in clinical research, again at Mount Sinai School of Medicine, further solidifying my expertise in the field. My journey then took me to Emory University, where I became the Director of Clinical Trials for Pediatrics, overseeing groundbreaking studies aimed at improving children's health outcomes.

In 2023, I achieved another milestone, completing my doctorate, a Ph.D. in Public Health from Walden University. It was a culmination of years of dedication, learning, and commitment to advancing health equity through research. My dissertation focused on positive social change through increasing representation in clinical research. Now, I have the privilege of serving as an Assistant Professor and Associate Director for Public Health at the University of Bridgeport, which happens to be my alma mater for my undergraduate degree. The opportunity to return to where it all began and shape the next generation of public health and clinical research professionals is truly a full-circle moment.

Beyond academia, I founded SpringWell360, a health equity company dedicated to raising awareness of clinical trials as a care option, particularly for underserved communities. I also have the exciting opportunity to launch courses designed to help others enter the field of clinical research and academia, paving the way for more diverse voices in research and education.

Overall, I landed in the field of public health and clinical research by accident. I never sought out to be a public health or clinical research professional in my high school or college days. However, I started working at an entry-level position in the field and worked my way up, from research assistant to clinical research coordinator, to research manager, to research director, to now as a professor and founder and CEO of my own company. It's the only field I've worked in. And I wouldn't change a thing about that. I'd love to make the field more accessible to those who want to enter clinical trials and make an impact.

Looking back, I never could have imagined where my love for science and problem-solving would take me. My journey into clinical research wasn't planned; it unfolded through curiosity, unexpected opportunities, and a desire to create meaningful change. Now, I am committed to helping others discover their path, ensuring that more people, especially those from underrepresented communities, have access to education, research opportunities, and life-changing clinical trials.

This is just the beginning.

CHAPTER 1

Introduction

Welcome to the world of clinical research, where science meets innovation, and discovery transforms into life-changing therapies. This field is at the forefront of medical advancement—every trial conducted, every data point collected, and every decision made plays a crucial role in improving patient outcomes and shaping the future of healthcare. In this book, we will take you on a comprehensive journey through the essential skills, strategies, and insights needed to excel in clinical research and carve out a rewarding, six-figure career. Whether you're a newcomer eager to break into the industry or a seasoned professional looking to advance, this guide will equip you with the tools to thrive in a competitive and rapidly evolving landscape.

We will explore the full spectrum of clinical research. From understanding study protocols and regulatory frameworks to mastering data analysis, patient engagement, and project management. You'll gain practical knowledge on how to navigate complex trials, ensure compliance with ethical standards, and contribute to groundbreaking medical innovations. More than just technical expertise, we'll also delve into the soft skills that set successful professionals apart—communication, adaptability, and the ability to work collaboratively across multidisciplinary teams.

But this book goes beyond the basics. You'll learn how to position yourself as a leader in clinical research, leverage opportunities for career growth, and strategically build a pathway to financial success. We'll also address critical issues such as health equity and the importance of diverse representation in clinical trials—an area where your work can make a lasting impact on underserved communities. Throughout these pages, you will find actionable insights, real-world examples, and proven strategies to help you stay ahead in this fast-paced field. By the end, you'll not only have the knowledge to succeed but also the confidence to pursue a meaningful career that drives scientific progress and transforms patient lives.

Your journey to mastering clinical research and unlocking a six-figure career starts here. Let's get started!

The Landscape of Clinical Research

Clinical research is the backbone of medical advancement. It encompasses a broad spectrum of activities from the initial discovery of a potential therapeutic agent to its introduction into the market as a new treatment option. The journey is complex and requires the collaboration of various professionals, including scientists, clinicians, regulatory experts, and statisticians, among others. Clinical research is not just about conducting trials; it is about asking the right questions, designing robust studies, collecting and analyzing data, and ensuring patient safety and regulatory compliance. This multifaceted field offers numerous career opportunities, each with its own set of challenges and rewards.

Clinical research stands as the cornerstone of medical advancement, driving the development of new therapies that have the potential to change lives. It's a field where science, innovation, and patient care converge, offering a pathway from the laboratory bench to the patient's bedside. Understanding the landscape of clinical research is essential for anyone entering this field, as it provides the context within which all research activities occur.

The journey of clinical research begins with the discovery of a potential therapeutic agent, often emerging from years of basic scientific research. Once a promising compound is identified, the journey toward becoming a marketable treatment involves a series of rigorous steps designed to ensure its safety and efficacy. This journey can be broadly categorized into several phases. First, there is the preclinical research phase. Before any new treatment is tested in humans, it undergoes extensive preclinical research, often in the form of laboratory and animal studies. These studies aim to understand the mechanism of action, potential efficacy, and safety profile of the compound. Positive results in preclinical research are a prerequisite for advancing to human trials.

Clinical Trials Phases I–IV follow. Phase I trials are the first step in testing a new treatment in humans. These small-scale studies focus on safety, dosage, and pharmacokinetics (how the drug is absorbed, distributed, metabolized, and excreted). Phase II trials expand the participant pool and aim to provide preliminary data on the treatment's efficacy, as well as continue to assess safety. Phase III trials are large-scale studies that involve a broader population and provide the most definitive evidence of efficacy and safety. These trials are critical for regulatory approval. Phase IV (post-marketing) studies are conducted after a treatment has been approved and is on the market. These studies continue to monitor the treatment's long-term effects and gather additional information on its use in the general population. Each of these phases requires the collaboration of a wide range of professionals, including scientists, clinicians, regulatory experts, biostatisticians, data managers, and more. The success of a clinical trial depends on the seamless integration of these diverse roles.

Regulatory bodies, such as the U.S. Food and Drug Administration (FDA) and the European Medicines Agency (EMA), play a pivotal role in overseeing clinical research. These agencies are responsible for ensuring that all clinical trials are conducted ethically and that the data generated is robust and reliable. They set the standards for trial design, patient safety, and data integrity, and they are the final gatekeepers in approving new treatments for market release.

Regulatory compliance is not just about following rules; it's about upholding the highest standards of patient safety and scientific integrity. Understanding the regulatory landscape is crucial for anyone involved in clinical research, as it influences every aspect of trial design, implementation, and reporting.

At the heart of clinical research is the study design. A well-designed study is essential for generating meaningful data that can answer key clinical questions. Study design involves careful consideration of various factors, including the selection of participants, the choice of endpoints (the outcomes used to measure the treatment's effect), and the statistical methods used to analyze the data. Study designs can vary widely, from randomized controlled trials (RCTs) to observational studies, each with its own strengths and limitations. RCTs are considered the gold standard in clinical research because they minimize bias and allow for causal inferences about the treatment's effects. However, not all research questions can be answered with an RCT, and other study designs may be more appropriate depending on the research objectives.

The collection and analysis of data are critical components of clinical research. High-quality data is the foundation of credible research findings. This process involves meticulous planning and execution, from the development of data collection tools to the implementation of data management systems that ensure accuracy, consistency, and completeness.

Biostatisticians play a key role in the analysis of clinical trial data, applying statistical methods to interpret the results and determine the significance of the findings. The interpretation of data must be done with care, as it forms the basis for decisions about the future of the treatment, including whether it will proceed to the next phase of development or be submitted for regulatory approval.

Patient safety is paramount in clinical research. Every aspect of a clinical trial is designed with the safety and well-being of participants in mind. This includes the informed consent process, where participants are fully educated about the risks and benefits of the study before agreeing to take part. It also involves ongoing monitoring of participants for adverse events throughout the trial. Ethical considerations are central to patient safety. The principles of respect for persons, beneficence, and justice guide all clinical research activities. Institutional Review Boards (IRBs) or Ethics Committees review study protocols to ensure that they are ethically sound and that the rights and welfare of participants are protected.

The Importance of Clinical Research

The impact of clinical research on healthcare cannot be overstated. It is through rigorous clinical studies that we understand the efficacy and safety of new drugs, medical devices, and treatment protocols. Clinical research drives medical innovation, leading to new treatments that improve patient outcomes and quality of life. For instance, the development of vaccines, cancer therapies, and novel diagnostic tools has been possible due to extensive clinical research. These advancements not only save lives but also enhance the overall efficiency and effectiveness of healthcare systems worldwide.

Clinical research serves as the backbone of modern medicine, driving advancements that shape the future of healthcare. From groundbreaking treatments to life-saving therapies, clinical research is essential in ensuring that medical interventions are safe, effective, and accessible to those who need them most. Without it, the healthcare field would stagnate, leaving millions of patients without innovative solutions for their conditions. At its core, clinical research is about discovery and uncovering new ways to diagnose, treat, and prevent diseases. It provides the scientific evidence needed to confirm whether a new drug, medical device, or therapy is both effective and safe for human use. Through carefully designed trials, researchers can determine how treatments interact with different populations, identify potential side effects, and refine medical interventions to maximize patient benefits.

For example, decades of clinical research have led to revolutionary breakthroughs in areas such as cancer treatment, cardiovascular disease management, and infectious disease prevention. The development of immunotherapies, which harness the body's immune system to fight cancer, is a direct result of clinical studies. Similarly, the rapid development and distribution of COVID-19 vaccines in response to a global pandemic underscored the vital role that clinical research plays in public health.

Clinical research does more than just advance science, it transforms lives. By participating in clinical trials, patients gain access to cutting-edge treatments that are not yet widely available. For those with life-threatening conditions, such as rare cancers or genetic disorders, clinical trials can provide hope where traditional treatments have failed.

In many cases, research has led to the development of therapies that significantly improve survival rates and quality of life. For instance, targeted therapies in oncology have enabled doctors to personalize cancer treatment based on a patient's genetic makeup, reducing harmful side effects and improving treatment success rates. Similarly, advancements in diabetes management, such as continuous glucose monitoring systems, have helped millions of patients better control their blood sugar levels, preventing complications and enhancing their daily lives.

One of the most critical aspects of clinical research is its role in addressing health disparities. Historically, many clinical trials have lacked diversity, leading to gaps in medical knowledge and treatments that do not adequately serve all populations. Without sufficient representation, certain racial, ethnic, and gender groups may be at risk of receiving less effective treatments due to differences in genetics, lifestyle, and environmental factors.

Efforts to improve diversity in clinical trials are essential in achieving health equity. By including participants from various backgrounds, researchers can ensure that new therapies work effectively across different populations, leading to more inclusive and personalized healthcare solutions. This is particularly important in diseases that disproportionately affect certain communities, such as sickle cell disease, which primarily impacts individuals of African descent.

Beyond individual patient benefits, clinical research has a profound impact on healthcare systems and economies. Medical advancements driven by research reduce hospitalizations, minimize healthcare costs, and enhance overall efficiency. For example, the introduction of minimally invasive surgical techniques—developed through extensive clinical studies—has led to shorter recovery times, reduced complications, and decreased healthcare expenditures. The clinical research industry itself creates jobs, fosters innovation, and strengthens economies. Pharmaceutical companies, research institutions, and healthcare organizations invest billions of dollars annually in research and development, driving economic growth while improving public health. Countries that prioritize clinical research also attract global investment, positioning themselves as leaders in medical innovation.

With great power comes great responsibility, and clinical research must be conducted with the highest ethical standards. Patient safety is paramount, and regulatory agencies such as the U.S. Food and Drug Administration (FDA) and the European Medicines Agency (EMA) enforce strict guidelines to ensure that trials are conducted ethically and transparently.

Informed consent, data privacy, and equitable treatment of all participants are fundamental to maintaining public trust in clinical research. Past medical injustices, such as the Tuskegee Syphilis Study, have left deep scars, leading to ongoing mistrust in certain communities. Addressing these concerns through ethical research practices, community engagement, and transparent communication is crucial in fostering trust and encouraging broader participation in clinical studies.

The future of healthcare depends on continued investment in clinical research. As technology advances, we can expect to see even greater innovations, such as precision medicine, artificial intelligence-driven drug discovery, and the expansion of decentralized clinical trials that increase access for patients in remote areas.

For clinical research to reach its full potential, it must remain patient-centered, diverse, and ethically sound. By prioritizing these principles, we can ensure that the next generation of medical breakthroughs benefits all individuals, regardless of background or geography. Clinical research is more than just a scientific endeavor—it is a commitment to improving human health, advancing equity, and transforming lives for generations to come.

Career Opportunities in Clinical Research

The multifaceted nature of clinical research offers numerous career opportunities, each with its own set of challenges and rewards. The field of clinical research offers a variety of career paths, each requiring specific skills and expertise. Whether your interest lies in clinical trial management, regulatory affairs, finance, data analysis, contracting, legal, or patient care, there is a role for you in this field.

Some key roles in clinical research include the clinical research associate, commonly known as the CRA, clinical project manager, regulatory affairs specialist, biostatistician, data manager, clinical research coordinator, clinical trial manager, and many more.

Clinical Research Associate (CRA): Responsible for monitoring the progress of clinical trials and ensuring that they are conducted in accordance with the protocol, Good Clinical Practice (GCP), and regulatory requirements.

Key Responsibilities:

☑ Trial Monitoring & Site Management:
- Conducts Site Initiation Visits (SIVs), Interim Monitoring Visits (IMVs), and Close-Out Visits (COVs) to ensure sites adhere to study protocols.
- Oversees patient recruitment, informed consent process, and data collection to confirm protocol compliance.
- Verifies that clinical sites maintain accurate and complete source documentation, case report forms (CRFs), and electronic data capture (EDC) entries.

☑ Regulatory & Compliance Oversight:
- Ensures all trial activities comply with ICH-GCP, FDA, EMA, and other regulatory guidelines.
- Confirms that clinical trial sites have necessary regulatory approvals, ethics committee approvals, and signed investigator agreements.
- Monitors adverse events (AEs) and serious adverse events (SAEs), ensuring proper documentation and timely reporting.

☑ Data Integrity & Quality Assurance:
- Conducts source data verification (SDV) to ensure accuracy and completeness of trial data.
- Identifies and resolves protocol deviations, discrepancies, and data queries in collaboration with site personnel.
- Assists in audits and inspections by regulatory agencies or sponsors.

☑ Site Training & Support:
- Provides training and ongoing support to investigators, coordinators, and site staff to ensure adherence to study procedures.
- Acts as a primary liaison between the sponsor/CRO and the clinical site, addressing challenges and facilitating smooth trial execution.

☑ Travel & Remote Monitoring:
- Frequently travels to clinical trial sites to conduct monitoring visits and ensure compliance.
- Adopts remote monitoring techniques, utilizing risk-based monitoring (RBM) approaches and centralized data review.

Skills & Qualifications:

- ✓ Scientific & Regulatory Knowledge – Understanding of GCP, clinical trial protocols, and regulatory requirements.
- ✓ Attention to Detail – Ability to identify data inconsistencies and protocol deviations.
- ✓ Communication & Interpersonal Skills – Strong relationship-building with site staff, sponsors, and regulatory bodies.
- ✓ Problem-Solving & Critical Thinking – Addressing challenges in trial execution and compliance.
- ✓ Project Management & Organization – Managing multiple trial sites efficiently.

Career Path & Growth:

- Entry-Level: Clinical Research Coordinator (CRC) → CRA I
- Mid-Level: CRA II → Senior CRA
- Advanced Roles: Lead CRA → Clinical Trial Manager (CTM) → Director of Clinical Operations

The role of a CRA is dynamic and essential to the success of clinical trials, ensuring that investigational treatments are tested safely, ethically, and effectively before reaching the market.

Clinical Project Manager (CPM): Oversees the planning, execution, and completion of clinical trials, managing timelines, budgets, and resources.

A Clinical Project Manager (CPM) plays a vital role in the successful planning, execution, and completion of clinical trials, ensuring that studies are conducted on time, within budget, and in compliance with Good Clinical Practice (GCP), regulatory guidelines, and sponsor expectations. CPMs serve as strategic leaders, coordinating cross-functional teams, mitigating risks, and ensuring smooth trial operations from start to finish.

Key Responsibilities:

☑ Study Planning & Trial Design:
- Develops comprehensive project plans, timelines, and key milestones for clinical trials.
- Defines study objectives, site selection strategy, and patient recruitment goals in collaboration with stakeholders.
- Works with cross-functional teams to ensure clinical trial protocols, informed consent forms (ICFs), and regulatory submissions are ready.

☑ Project Execution & Oversight:
- Leads and manages clinical research teams, vendors, and CROs to ensure timely and efficient trial execution.
- Monitors trial progress, patient enrollment, site performance, and protocol compliance to prevent delays.
- Ensures adherence to Standard Operating Procedures (SOPs), GCP, and regulatory requirements (FDA, EMA, ICH guidelines, etc.).

☑ Budget & Resource Management:
- Develops and manages clinical trial budgets, ensuring cost efficiency and alignment with financial plans.
- Oversees vendor selection, contract negotiations, and resource allocation, including monitoring staff workloads.
- Tracks study expenditures, forecasts budget needs, and ensures cost control throughout the trial.

☑ Risk Management & Problem-Solving:
- Identifies and mitigates potential risks, such as regulatory delays, patient recruitment challenges, and data integrity issues.

- Implements corrective and preventive actions (CAPA) to address trial deviations and compliance concerns.
- Works closely with Data Management and Safety Monitoring Committees to ensure patient safety and trial integrity.

☑ Stakeholder Communication & Reporting:
- Serves as the primary point of contact between sponsors, CROs, regulatory agencies, and clinical sites.
- Provides regular study updates, risk assessments, and performance metrics to leadership and sponsors.
- Facilitates investigator meetings, study training sessions, and cross-functional team discussions to align trial objectives.

☑ Regulatory Compliance & Quality Assurance:
- Ensures that all clinical trial activities comply with ICH-GCP, FDA, EMA, and local regulatory requirements.
- Collaborates with Quality Assurance (QA) teams to support audits, inspections, and compliance reviews.
- Oversees the development of Trial Master Files (TMF) and essential regulatory documents.

☑ Study Close-Out & Reporting:
- Ensures timely database lock, clinical study report (CSR) development, and regulatory submissions.
- Oversees site closure activities, final budget reconciliation, and post-study audits.
- Assists in lessons learned and continuous process improvement for future clinical trials.

Essential Skills & Qualifications:

- ✓ Project Management & Leadership – Ability to coordinate multiple teams, vendors, and stakeholders.
- ✓ Strategic Thinking & Decision-Making – Anticipating challenges and implementing proactive solutions.
- ✓ Budget & Financial Acumen – Managing study costs, contracts, and financial planning.
- ✓ Regulatory Knowledge – Understanding of FDA, EMA, ICH-GCP, and country-specific requirements.
- ✓ Strong Communication & Negotiation – Liaising with sponsors, CROs, and clinical sites.
- ✓ Risk Assessment & Problem-Solving – Addressing study issues and ensuring trial continuity.

Career Path & Growth:

- Entry-Level: Clinical Research Associate (CRA) → Clinical Trial Lead (CTL)
- Mid-Level: Clinical Project Manager (CPM) → Senior Clinical Project Manager
- Advanced Roles: Director of Clinical Operations → VP of Clinical Development → Chief Clinical Officer

The Clinical Project Manager is a critical leadership role in clinical research, ensuring that trials progress efficiently, safely, and in compliance with global regulations, ultimately bringing innovative therapies to market.

Regulatory Affairs Specialist: Regulatory Affairs Specialist focuses on ensuring that clinical trials and new treatments comply with all regulatory requirements and are successfully submitted for approval.

A Regulatory Affairs Specialist plays a crucial role in the clinical research and drug development process, ensuring that clinical trials, investigational products, and new treatments comply with all local, national, and international regulatory requirements. This professional acts as the bridge between pharmaceutical companies, contract research organizations (CROs), medical device firms, and regulatory agencies (such as the FDA, EMA, MHRA, and Health Canada) to facilitate the approval and commercialization of new therapies.

Key Responsibilities:

✅ Regulatory Compliance & Strategy Development:
- Ensures that all clinical trial protocols, study designs, and investigational products comply with applicable regulations.
- Advises cross-functional teams on regulatory strategies to expedite approval timelines and mitigate risks.
- Keeps up to date with changing regulatory guidelines (e.g., ICH-GCP, FDA 21 CFR, EMA Clinical Trial Regulation, ISO standards for medical devices).

✅ Regulatory Submissions & Approvals:
- Prepares, reviews, and submits Investigational New Drug (IND) applications, Clinical Trial Applications (CTAs), Biologic License Applications (BLAs), New Drug Applications (NDAs), and Medical Device Submissions (510(k), PMA).
- Coordinates with regulatory agencies to obtain approvals for clinical trials, marketing authorizations, and product labeling.
- Responds to agency inquiries, deficiency letters, and audit findings to ensure continuous compliance.

✅ Clinical Trial Oversight & Documentation:
- Ensures that clinical trials adhere to Good Clinical Practice (GCP), Institutional Review Board (IRB)/Ethics Committee requirements, and regulatory approvals.
- Oversees the preparation and maintenance of Regulatory Binders, Trial Master Files (TMFs), and essential documents required for audits and inspections.
- Collaborates with Clinical Operations teams to monitor regulatory compliance throughout the trial.

✅ Liaison with Regulatory Authorities:
- Serves as the primary point of contact between sponsors, CROs, and health authorities (FDA, EMA, MHRA, Health Canada, TGA, etc.).
- Participates in regulatory meetings (e.g., Pre-IND, End-of-Phase 2, and Pre-NDA meetings) to facilitate drug development discussions.
- Prepares responses to regulatory queries and assists with regulatory inspections and audits.

✅ Labeling, Advertising & Post-Market Compliance:
- Ensures that product labeling, advertising, and promotional materials comply with FDA, EMA, and other global regulatory requirements.
- Supports post-market surveillance, risk management, and pharmacovigilance reporting for approved products.
- Assists in post-approval changes, renewals, and variations to marketing authorizations.

✅ Regulatory Intelligence & Risk Management:
- Monitors global regulatory trends, policy changes, and new industry regulations to inform business decisions.

- Conducts regulatory risk assessments and provides guidance on strategies to overcome compliance challenges.
- Works closely with Quality Assurance (QA) teams to ensure compliance with GMP (Good Manufacturing Practices) and GLP (Good Laboratory Practices).

Essential Skills & Qualifications:

✓ In-Depth Regulatory Knowledge – Understanding of FDA, EMA, ICH-GCP, and country-specific regulations.

✓ Strong Technical Writing & Documentation – Preparing precise and well-organized regulatory submissions.

✓ Attention to Detail & Analytical Thinking – Ensuring accuracy in regulatory documents and risk assessments.

✓ Project Management & Coordination – Managing multiple regulatory submissions and deadlines.

✓ Communication & Negotiation – Engaging with health authorities, internal teams, and external stakeholders.

✓ Adaptability & Problem-Solving – Navigating evolving regulatory landscapes and addressing compliance challenges.

Career Path & Growth:

- Entry-Level: Regulatory Affairs Associate → Regulatory Affairs Specialist
- Mid-Level: Senior Regulatory Affairs Specialist → Regulatory Affairs Manager
- Advanced Roles: Director of Regulatory Affairs → VP of Regulatory Strategy → Chief Regulatory Officer

The Regulatory Affairs Specialist is a critical role in ensuring that new drugs, biologics, and medical devices reach the market efficiently and safely while adhering to global regulatory standards. Their work directly impacts the speed and success of clinical trials and product approvals, making them indispensable in the healthcare and pharmaceutical industries.

Biostatistician: Applies statistical methods to design studies and analyze data, providing critical insights into the efficacy and safety of treatments. A Biostatistician plays a key role in clinical research and public health by applying statistical methods to design studies, analyze data, and draw meaningful conclusions about the efficacy, safety, and impact of medical treatments and interventions. Their work ensures that clinical trials generate reliable and scientifically valid results, which are crucial for regulatory approvals and medical decision-making.

Key Responsibilities:

☑ Study Design & Statistical Planning:

- Develops the statistical methodology for clinical trials, ensuring proper randomization, sample size determination, and power calculations.
- Designs and implements statistical analysis plans (SAPs) that define how trial data will be analyzed and interpreted.
- Works closely with clinical researchers to identify appropriate endpoints and hypothesis testing strategies.

☑ Data Analysis & Interpretation:

- Applies advanced statistical techniques (e.g., regression analysis, survival analysis, Bayesian modeling, machine learning) to assess treatment outcomes.
- Conducts interim and final analyses to monitor trial progress and determine whether a study should continue or be modified.

- Interprets complex datasets to provide insights on treatment efficacy, safety profiles, and potential adverse events.

✅ Regulatory Compliance & Reporting:

- Prepares statistical reports and Clinical Study Reports (CSRs) for submission to regulatory agencies (e.g., FDA, EMA).
- Ensures compliance with regulatory requirements, including ICH-GCP, CDISC (Clinical Data Interchange Standards Consortium), and regulatory guidelines on statistical analysis.
- Provides statistical justifications and responses to regulatory agencies during drug approval processes.

✅ Collaboration with Cross-Functional Teams:

- Works with clinical investigators, epidemiologists, and data managers to ensure accurate data collection and interpretation.
- Supports sponsor companies, CROs, and regulatory authorities with statistical expertise during protocol development and review meetings.
- Provides input on manuscripts, publications, and conference presentations to disseminate research findings.

Essential Skills & Qualifications:

- ✓ Expertise in SAS, R, Python, or STATA for statistical computing and data visualization.
- ✓ Strong foundation in probability theory, experimental design, and hypothesis testing.
- ✓ Ability to translate complex statistical results into meaningful conclusions for non-statistical stakeholders.
- ✓ Knowledge of clinical trial design, epidemiology, and regulatory guidelines.

✓ Attention to detail and the ability to identify patterns and trends in large datasets.

Career Path & Growth:

- Entry-Level: Biostatistical Analyst → Biostatistician
- Mid-Level: Senior Biostatistician → Principal Biostatistician
- Advanced Roles: Director of Biostatistics → VP of Biometrics → Chief Data Science Officer

Biostatisticians play a crucial role in evidence-based medicine, helping researchers make data-driven decisions that improve patient outcomes and advance medical science.

<u>Data Manager</u>: Responsible for overseeing the collection, storage, quality control, and security of data generated in clinical trials. They ensure that all data is accurate, complete, and regulatory-compliant, which is essential for drawing valid conclusions about treatment efficacy and safety.

Key Responsibilities:

☑ Clinical Data Collection & Management:
- Designs and maintains Clinical Data Management Systems (CDMS) to efficiently capture and store trial data.
- Develops Case Report Forms (CRFs) and ensures that data is entered correctly and consistently.
- Manages electronic data capture (EDC) platforms such as Medidata Rave, Oracle Clinical, and REDCap.

☑ Data Quality Assurance & Integrity:
- Implements data validation procedures, query resolution, and discrepancy management to ensure high-quality datasets.

- Conducts data cleaning, coding, and standardization to meet regulatory and sponsor requirements.
- Works closely with data entry personnel and site coordinators to ensure compliance with study protocols.

✓ Regulatory Compliance & Audit Preparation:
- Ensures that data collection and management processes follow ICH-GCP, CDISC, and 21 CFR Part 11 guidelines.
- Prepares for audits and inspections by maintaining accurate and complete data documentation.
- Supports the generation of clinical trial reports, safety reports, and regulatory submissions.

✓ Collaboration with Clinical & Biostatistics Teams:
- Works closely with Clinical Research Associates (CRAs), Biostatisticians, and Regulatory Affairs Specialists to ensure smooth data flow and compliance.
- Assists in the development of data analysis plans and the interpretation of clinical trial results.
- Provides training to study teams on data management best practices.

Essential Skills & Qualifications:

✓ Expertise in clinical data management software (e.g., Medidata, Oracle Clinical, OpenClinica).

✓ Strong knowledge of CDISC standards (SDTM, ADaM) and regulatory data requirements.

✓ Ability to identify and resolve data discrepancies and ensure data consistency.

✓ Understanding of database programming (SQL, SAS, Python) for data extraction and cleaning.

✓ Strong problem-solving skills and the ability to manage large datasets efficiently.

Career Path & Growth:

- Entry-Level: Clinical Data Coordinator → Clinical Data Manager
- Mid-Level: Senior Data Manager → Lead Data Manager
- Advanced Roles: Director of Clinical Data Management → VP of Data Operations → Chief Data Officer

Data Managers are critical to ensuring the success and reliability of clinical trials, providing high-quality data that informs regulatory decisions, medical advancements, and patient care improvements.

Clinical Research Coordinator (CRC): Responsible for overseeing clinical trials, ensuring compliance with regulatory requirements, and managing data collection.

A Clinical Research Coordinator (CRC) is a key professional in clinical trials, responsible for managing day-to-day trial operations at a research site. CRCs ensure that studies are conducted in compliance with protocols, regulatory guidelines, and Good Clinical Practice (GCP) while prioritizing patient safety and data integrity. They serve as the primary point of contact between the research site, study participants, sponsors, and regulatory authorities.

Key Responsibilities:

☑ Study Coordination & Protocol Compliance:
- Manages and oversees the execution of clinical trials according to study protocols, ensuring adherence to GCP, FDA, and IRB (Institutional Review Board) regulations.

- Works closely with Principal Investigators (PIs) and study teams to implement study procedures and maintain compliance.
- Ensures that inclusion/exclusion criteria are strictly followed to enroll eligible participants.

☑ Patient Recruitment, Consent & Retention:
- Identifies, recruits, and screens potential clinical trial participants based on protocol requirements.
- Educates participants about the study risks, benefits, and expectations, obtaining informed consent as required by ethical guidelines.
- Implements patient retention strategies to minimize dropout rates and ensure the trial's success.

☑ Data Collection, Management & Reporting:
- Collects, records, and enters accurate clinical data into Case Report Forms (CRFs) or Electronic Data Capture (EDC) systems such as Medidata Rave, REDCap, or Oracle Clinical.
- Ensures data accuracy, integrity, and completeness by performing source data verification (SDV) and resolving data queries.
- Assists with adverse event (AE) and serious adverse event (SAE) reporting, ensuring timely submission to regulatory bodies.

☑ Regulatory & Ethical Compliance:
- Works with the Institutional Review Board (IRB) to submit and maintain study approvals.
- Maintains up-to-date regulatory documentation, including informed consent forms, investigator brochures, and protocol amendments.
- Ensures compliance with ICH-GCP, FDA, and HIPAA regulations regarding participant confidentiality and ethical research practices.

☑ Collaboration with Sponsors, Monitors & Study Teams:
- Acts as a liaison between the research site, study sponsors, Contract Research Organizations (CROs), and regulatory agencies.
- Prepares for and participates in site monitoring visits, sponsor audits, and FDA inspections.
- Supports Clinical Research Associates (CRAs) during Site Initiation Visits (SIVs), Interim Monitoring Visits (IMVs), and Close-Out Visits (COVs).

☑ Study Logistics & Budget Management:
- Coordinates the ordering, storage, and administration of investigational products (IP) and laboratory supplies.
- Helps manage study budgets, site payments, and participant reimbursement.
- Ensures that all study activities are conducted within timelines and financial constraints.

Essential Skills & Qualifications:

- ✓ Strong organizational and multitasking abilities to manage multiple studies and patient interactions.
- ✓ Knowledge of clinical trial phases, regulatory requirements, and ethical considerations.
- ✓ Proficiency in data management tools (EDC systems, CTMS, and Microsoft Office Suite).
- ✓ Excellent interpersonal and communication skills to interact with participants, study teams, and regulatory bodies.
- ✓ Ability to identify and resolve compliance issues while maintaining study integrity.

Career Path & Growth:

- Entry-Level: Research Assistant → Clinical Research Coordinator (CRC)
- Mid-Level: Senior CRC → Clinical Trial Manager (CTM) → Clinical Project Manager (CPM)
- Advanced Roles: Director of Clinical Operations → VP of Clinical Research → Chief Scientific Officer

Clinical Research Coordinators are the backbone of clinical trials, ensuring that research is conducted ethically, efficiently, and in compliance with regulations while advancing medical innovation and improving patient care.

Clinical Trial Manager (CTM): Manages all aspects of clinical trials, from planning and initiation to completion and reporting.

A Clinical Trial Manager (CTM) is a key leadership role in the clinical research industry, overseeing the entire lifecycle of a clinical trial from planning and initiation to execution, completion, and reporting. They ensure that trials are conducted on time, within budget, and in compliance with regulatory requirements while maintaining high-quality standards. CTMs serve as a bridge between sponsors, Contract Research Organizations (CROs), study sites, and regulatory agencies, ensuring smooth trial operations.

Key Responsibilities:

☑ Clinical Trial Planning & Study Design:
- Collaborates with sponsors, investigators, and regulatory teams to develop study protocols and trial designs that align with scientific objectives and regulatory guidelines.

- Oversees the preparation of study plans, timelines, budgets, and resource allocation to ensure trials run efficiently.
- Works with regulatory affairs specialists to submit necessary documentation (e.g., IND, CTA, IRB submissions) before trial initiation.

☑ Site Selection, Initiation & Monitoring:
- Identifies and selects investigator sites that meet the study's requirements, ensuring appropriate infrastructure, experience, and patient population.
- Oversees Site Initiation Visits (SIVs) to train investigators, study coordinators, and research staff on study protocols, Good Clinical Practice (GCP), and regulatory expectations.
- Works closely with Clinical Research Associates (CRAs) to ensure proper monitoring of site activities, including compliance with protocols and data integrity.

☑ Trial Execution & Oversight:
- Ensures timely patient enrollment and retention strategies to meet study recruitment goals.
- Monitors clinical trial progress, resolving operational issues and ensuring that all stakeholders are aligned with study objectives.
- Oversees investigational product (IP) supply chain management, ensuring that study drugs are distributed and maintained according to protocol and regulatory requirements.

☑ Regulatory Compliance & Risk Management:
- Ensures all trial activities comply with ICH-GCP, FDA, EMA, MHRA, and other global regulatory agencies.
- Works with compliance teams to mitigate risks related to patient safety, data integrity, and ethical concerns.

- Supports regulatory inspections, audits, and sponsor reviews, ensuring proper documentation and adherence to study procedures.

✅ Data Management & Quality Assurance:
- Oversees data collection, validation, and submission to ensure accurate and high-quality results.
- Works closely with biostatisticians and data managers to analyze trial data and ensure compliance with reporting requirements.
- Ensures prompt identification and reporting of adverse events (AEs) and serious adverse events (SAEs) per regulatory guidelines.

✅ Budget & Resource Management:
- Manages clinical trial budgets, tracking expenses, contracts, and vendor agreements to ensure cost efficiency.
- Works with CROs, sponsors, and vendors to optimize site payments, contract negotiations, and resource allocation.
- Ensures that trials stay within financial constraints while maintaining quality and regulatory compliance.

✅ Study Close-Out & Reporting:
- Manages trial completion activities, ensuring that final patient visits, data cleaning, and statistical analyses are completed efficiently.
- Works with regulatory teams to prepare Clinical Study Reports (CSRs) and submit findings to regulatory authorities.
- Ensures that trial results are documented, published, and shared with stakeholders in accordance with ethical standards.

Essential Skills & Qualifications:

- ✓ Strong leadership and project management skills to oversee multiple trial activities and teams.
- ✓ In-depth knowledge of clinical research regulations, including GCP, FDA, EMA, and IRB guidelines.
- ✓ Experience in site monitoring, patient recruitment, and protocol compliance.
- ✓ Proficiency in clinical trial management systems (CTMS), electronic data capture (EDC) systems, and risk-based monitoring approaches.
- ✓ Ability to handle high-pressure situations, solve problems, and drive trial success.
- ✓ Excellent communication and stakeholder management skills to collaborate with sponsors, investigators, and regulatory agencies.

Career Path & Growth:

- Entry-Level: Clinical Research Associate (CRA) → Senior CRA
- Mid-Level: Clinical Trial Manager (CTM) → Clinical Project Manager (CPM)
- Advanced Roles: Director of Clinical Operations → VP of Clinical Research → Chief Operating Officer (COO)

A Clinical Trial Manager plays a critical role in the success of clinical trials, ensuring that new treatments and therapies reach patients safely and efficiently. Their leadership is essential in maintaining study integrity, patient safety, and regulatory compliance while driving forward groundbreaking medical advancements.

Clinical Trial Participant Recruiter: A Clinical Trial Participant Recruiter plays a critical role in the successful execution of clinical research studies by identifying, engaging, and enrolling eligible individuals into clinical trials. With a deep understanding of inclusion/exclusion criteria, community outreach strategies, and regulatory compliance, this professional ensures that trials are representative, ethically conducted, and completed on time.

Participant recruiters may work at academic research centers, hospitals, site management organizations (SMOs), Contract Research Organizations (CROs), or directly with pharmaceutical and biotechnology sponsors.

Key Responsibilities:

✅ Participant Identification & Eligibility Screening
- Develops and implements strategies to identify potential participants who meet trial-specific inclusion and exclusion criteria.
- Conducts pre-screening interviews to gather relevant medical history and determine initial eligibility.
- Collaborates with clinical staff to ensure accurate assessment and documentation of participant data.

✅ Community Outreach & Engagement
- Builds relationships with community organizations, clinics, advocacy groups, and local health providers to promote clinical trial opportunities.
- Hosts or supports community events, webinars, and informational sessions to educate the public about clinical research participation.
- Focuses on inclusive recruitment strategies to reach underrepresented populations, improving trial diversity and health equity.

☑ Patient Communication & Retention

- Provides clear and compassionate communication to potential participants regarding the clinical trial process, benefits, risks, and expectations.
- Maintains regular contact with enrollees to reduce dropout rates and ensure protocol adherence.
- Supports retention by addressing barriers such as transportation, scheduling, and trust.

☑ Recruitment Campaign Management

- Designs and manages targeted advertising and outreach campaigns through digital media, flyers, radio, and social media.
- Monitors campaign performance, adjusts outreach tactics, and reports on recruitment metrics.
- Partners with marketing teams and recruitment vendors to ensure messaging aligns with trial goals and patient needs.

☑ Collaboration with Study Teams & Sponsors

- Works closely with Principal Investigators, Study Coordinators, and CROs to align on enrollment targets and timelines.
- Participates in site feasibility assessments and contributes to realistic recruitment planning during trial startup.
- Communicates regularly with sponsors regarding recruitment progress, challenges, and mitigation strategies.

☑ Compliance & Documentation

- Ensures all recruitment activities are conducted in accordance with Good Clinical Practice (GCP), IRB-approved protocols, and HIPAA/privacy regulations.
- Maintains accurate records of outreach activities, pre-screening logs, and participant communication.

- Prepares for audits and monitors documentation for quality and regulatory compliance.

Essential Skills & Qualifications:

✓ Knowledge of Clinical Trials – Familiarity with clinical research processes, study protocols, and ethical guidelines

✓ Community Engagement – Experience building trust and rapport with diverse and underserved communities

✓ Communication & Cultural Competency – Ability to explain complex medical information in layperson terms across different populations

✓ Organizational Skills – Proficient in managing multiple recruitment campaigns, databases, and timelines

✓ Tech & Tools Proficiency – Skilled in using clinical trial management systems (CTMS), EHR data, REDCap, and CRM platforms

✓ Empathy & Advocacy – Committed to supporting potential participants with respect, transparency, and care

Career Path & Growth:

- Entry-Level: Recruitment Assistant → Clinical Recruitment Coordinator
- Mid-Level: Clinical Trial Recruiter → Participant Engagement Specialist
- Advanced Roles: Senior Patient Recruitment Manager → Director of Participant Recruitment & Engagement → VP of Clinical Trial Diversity & Inclusion

Clinical Research Contracts Specialist: A Clinical Research Contracts Specialist plays a critical role in supporting the legal, financial, and operational aspects of clinical trials by reviewing, drafting, negotiating, and managing clinical research agreements (CRAs), confidentiality agreements (CDAs), budget documents, and other essential contracts. This role ensures that clinical trials are conducted in compliance with institutional policies, sponsor requirements, applicable laws, and ethical standards.

The Contracts Specialist acts as a liaison between sponsors, CROs, legal departments, and research sites to facilitate timely study start-up and mitigate legal and financial risks to the organization.

Key Responsibilities:

☑ Contract Review & Negotiation
- Reviews and negotiates Clinical Trial Agreements (CTAs), Master Service Agreements (MSAs), Confidentiality Disclosure Agreements (CDAs), and amendments.
- Ensures contract terms align with regulatory requirements, institutional policies, and study budgets.
- Negotiates terms related to subject injury, indemnification, publication rights, and intellectual property.

☑ Collaboration & Communication
- Works closely with clinical operations, legal teams, principal investigators (PIs), finance teams, and sponsors/CROs to align on timelines and deliverables.
- Communicates changes, risks, and status updates to stakeholders.
- Facilitates communication between site and sponsor legal teams to expedite contract execution.

☑ Study Start-Up & Budget Integration
- Collaborates with start-up teams to ensure timely contract finalization in line with site activation goals.
- May assist in aligning contract terms with negotiated study budgets or payment schedules.
- Tracks contract milestones and timelines to prevent delays in patient recruitment.

☑ Compliance & Risk Management
- Ensures all contractual language complies with HIPAA, FDA, OHRP, and local/international regulatory bodies.
- Identifies and resolves contract-related risks to avoid future legal or financial disputes.
- Maintains awareness of institutional risk thresholds and sponsor preferences.

☑ Contract Tracking & Documentation
- Maintains accurate records of contract status, version history, and approval workflows.
- Supports audit readiness by ensuring all executed documents are properly archived in CTMS or contract management systems.
- May assist with contract reporting, KPIs, or metrics for internal and sponsor-facing dashboards.

Essential Skills & Qualifications:

- ✓ Contract Law & Clinical Trial Knowledge – Familiarity with legal terms related to clinical research, intellectual property, and human subject protection.
- ✓ Negotiation & Communication Skills – Able to balance the interests of multiple stakeholders while maintaining a collaborative tone.

✓ Attention to Detail & Organization – Precision in redlining contracts, tracking clauses, and managing timelines.

✓ Project Management Abilities – Capable of handling multiple studies and contracts simultaneously in a fast-paced environment.

✓ Tech Savvy – Proficiency with contract lifecycle management tools, CTMS, and Microsoft Office Suite.

✓ Regulatory & Ethical Understanding – Awareness of GCP, FDA, GDPR, and IRB requirements as they relate to research contracts.

Ideal Background:

- Bachelor's degree in Life Sciences, Legal Studies, Business Administration, or related field
- 2–5 years of experience reviewing and managing clinical research contracts (site, sponsor, CRO, or academic setting)
- Knowledge of clinical trial budgeting, finance, or grant management is a plus
- Paralegal certification, JD, or contract law coursework is a bonus but not required

Director of Clinical Research: A Director of Clinical Research leads and oversees the strategic planning, execution, and management of clinical trials to ensure the development of safe, effective, and compliant therapies. This senior-level role is pivotal in bridging scientific discovery and product approval by aligning clinical trial operations with regulatory standards, corporate goals, and patient needs.

The Director of Clinical Research serves as a key decision-maker and collaborator with cross-functional teams including Clinical Operations, Regulatory Affairs, Biostatistics, Data Management, and Medical Affairs. This individual ensures the design and delivery of high-quality, cost-effective, and timely clinical programs that support regulatory submissions and commercialization efforts.

Key Responsibilities:

✅ Strategic Leadership & Clinical Development Planning
- Leads the design and execution of clinical development plans (CDPs) aligned with regulatory pathways and corporate objectives.
- Oversees multiple clinical programs across phases (I–IV), including investigator-initiated trials and post-marketing studies.
- Evaluates therapeutic area trends, competitor strategies, and scientific advancements to inform protocol development and study design.

✅ Clinical Trial Oversight & Quality Assurance
- Ensures trials are conducted in accordance with ICH-GCP, FDA, EMA, and other global regulatory standards.
- Provides oversight for site selection, patient recruitment strategies, study start-up activities, and data collection processes.
- Collaborates with Clinical Operations, CROs, and vendors to meet quality, timeline, and budget goals.

✅ Cross-Functional Collaboration & Team Management
- Leads and mentors clinical research teams, including Clinical Project Managers, CRAs, and Study Coordinators.
- Partners with Biostatistics, Data Management, Pharmacovigilance, and Medical Writing to ensure cohesive execution and reporting of clinical trials.
- Facilitates communication between internal leadership and external stakeholders (investigators, KOLs, and regulatory agencies).

✅ Regulatory & Ethical Compliance
- Supports preparation of clinical sections for INDs, CTAs, NDAs, BLAs, and global regulatory filings.
- Ensures compliance with IRB/Ethics Committee submissions and approvals across study sites.
- Leads clinical input during regulatory meetings and inspections.

✅ Budget Management & Vendor Oversight
- Manages clinical research budgets, forecasts costs, and ensures resource allocation efficiency.
- Selects and oversees CROs, labs, and technology partners involved in trial execution.
- Evaluates vendor performance and negotiates service contracts.

✅ Risk Mitigation & Operational Excellence
- Identifies and mitigates risks across clinical programs through proactive planning and real-time monitoring.
- Implements systems for performance tracking, issue resolution, and continuous improvement.
- Promotes innovation through the integration of decentralized trial technologies, EHR data, and real-world evidence (RWE).

Essential Skills & Qualifications:

- ✓ Clinical Research Expertise – Deep knowledge of ICH-GCP, FDA, EMA, and global regulatory requirements across all phases of trials
- ✓ Leadership & Strategic Thinking – Proven ability to guide teams and align clinical programs with business goals
- ✓ Project Management Excellence – Skilled in leading large-scale, cross-functional clinical initiatives from start to finish

✓ Budget & Resource Management – Competence in managing multimillion-dollar budgets and optimizing vendor performance

✓ Strong Communication & Influence – Ability to effectively communicate with executive leadership, investigators, and partners

✓ Adaptability & Innovation – Embraces evolving technologies and patient-centric trial models

Career Path & Growth:

- Early Career: Clinical Research Associate → Clinical Trial Manager
- Mid-Level: Associate Director of Clinical Research → Director of Clinical Research
- Advanced Roles: Senior Director → VP of Clinical Development → Chief Medical/Clinical Officer (CMO/CCO)

Each of these roles requires a unique set of skills and offers different pathways for career advancement. The field of clinical research is constantly evolving, with new challenges and opportunities emerging as science and technology advance. Each of these roles is critical to the success of clinical research, and professionals in these positions can expect rewarding careers both intellectually and financially. For those who are passionate about science, patient care, and making a difference in the world, clinical research offers a fulfilling and impactful career path. There are so many more roles in clinical research, such as legal and epidemiology roles. If you want to work in clinical research and have a unique skill set, there is likely a niche for you.

A career in clinical research is both challenging and rewarding. The challenges are significant. There are complex protocols, regulatory hurdles, and the need for meticulous attention to detail. But the rewards are equally profound. There is satisfaction in contributing to the development of new therapies that can improve or save lives. There is also the opportunity for continuous learning and growth, as the field is ever-changing.

As we move forward in this book, we'll delve deeper into the specific skills, strategies, and insights needed to excel in each of these areas. Whether you're just starting out or looking to advance your career, understanding the landscape of clinical research is the first step on your journey to success.

Skills and Competencies Required

Success in clinical research requires a diverse set of skills and competencies. Some of the essential skills include:

- A strong foundation in biology, pharmacology, and medicine is crucial for understanding the principles underlying clinical research.
- Precision is key in clinical research, as even minor errors can compromise the validity of a study.
- The ability to manage time, resources, and tasks efficiently is vital for the smooth execution of clinical trials.
- Effective communication skills are essential for interacting with study participants, colleagues, and regulatory authorities.
- Understanding the regulatory environment and compliance requirements is critical for ensuring that clinical trials are conducted ethically and legally.
- The ability to analyze and interpret complex data is necessary for making informed decisions about the safety and efficacy of treatments.

Navigating the Regulatory Landscape

The regulatory environment in clinical research is stringent and continually evolving. Regulatory agencies such as the U.S. Food and Drug Administration (FDA) and the European Medicines Agency (EMA) set the standards for conducting clinical trials. Understanding these regulations and ensuring compliance is crucial for the success of any clinical study. This book will guide you through the regulatory requirements for clinical research, helping you navigate the complexities and avoid common pitfalls. You will learn about Good Clinical Practice (GCP) guidelines, the importance of ethical considerations, and the process of obtaining regulatory approvals.

The Role of Innovation in Clinical Research

Innovation is at the heart of clinical research. From the development of new study designs to the integration of advanced technologies like artificial intelligence and machine learning, innovation drives the field forward. Embracing new methodologies and tools can enhance the efficiency and effectiveness of clinical trials, leading to faster and more accurate results. In this book, we will explore the latest trends and innovations in clinical research, providing you with insights into how you can leverage these advancements in your own career.

Building a Successful Career in Clinical Research

Achieving a successful career in clinical research requires more than just technical knowledge; it involves continuous learning, networking, and professional development. This book will offer practical advice on how to build and sustain a career in this dynamic field. You will learn how to create a compelling résumé, prepare for interviews, and build a professional network. Additionally, we will discuss the importance of certifications and continuing education in advancing your career. The journey through the world of clinical research is challenging but immensely rewarding. By mastering the skills, strategies, and insights presented in this book, you will be well-equipped to navigate the complexities of clinical research and achieve a successful and lucrative career.

Welcome to the world of clinical research, where your contributions can make a significant impact on healthcare and improve the lives of patients around the globe. Let's embark on this journey together, exploring the pathways to mastering clinical research and unlocking the potential for a six-figure career.

CHAPTER 2

The Foundations of Clinical Research

C linical research is the structured process of investigating human health and disease with the goal of improving medical knowledge and developing new treatments. Unlike basic research, which typically takes place in a laboratory setting and focuses on understanding fundamental biological processes, clinical research is specifically concerned with testing the effectiveness, safety, and overall impact of medical interventions on human subjects. This includes a wide range of activities, from early-phase clinical trials that explore the safety and dosage of new drugs to large-scale, multi-center studies that confirm the efficacy of a treatment in diverse populations.

At its core, clinical research is about applying scientific methods to answer critical questions related to human health. This involves designing studies that are carefully structured to test specific hypotheses, collecting and analyzing data in a systematic manner, and interpreting the results to draw meaningful conclusions. The findings from clinical research are essential for guiding clinical practice, informing regulatory decisions, and shaping public health policies.

One of the most well-known aspects of clinical research is its role in drug development. This process involves several phases of clinical trials, each designed to answer specific questions about a new drug's safety, efficacy, and optimal use. Clinical trials are essential for determining whether a new drug should be approved for use by the general public.

Clinical research is also critical in the development and validation of medical devices and diagnostic tools. Like drug development, this involves rigorous testing to ensure that the device or diagnostic method is both safe and effective for its intended use. This can range from simple devices, such as glucose monitors, to complex technologies like MRI machines or surgical robots.

Beyond drugs and devices, clinical research also investigates the impact of behavioral and lifestyle interventions on health outcomes. This might include studies on the effectiveness of diet and exercise programs for managing chronic diseases or the use of cognitive-behavioral therapy for treating mental health conditions. These studies often require a different approach to trial design and data collection, reflecting the complex nature of human behavior.

Epidemiology, the study of how diseases affect populations, is another important area within clinical research. Epidemiological studies help to identify risk factors for disease, understand patterns of disease spread, and evaluate the effectiveness of public health interventions. These studies are critical for guiding public health policies and preventing disease outbreaks.

This area of clinical research focuses on evaluating the effectiveness, efficiency, and equity of health care services. Health services research examines how different healthcare practices, policies, and organizational structures affect patient outcomes and overall healthcare quality. The goal is to identify ways to improve the delivery of healthcare and ensure that all patients have access to high-quality care.

Given this wide scope, clinical research is inherently interdisciplinary, requiring collaboration among various professionals, including scientists, clinicians, statisticians, data managers, and regulatory experts.

Each of these roles brings a unique perspective and set of skills that contribute to the successful design, implementation, and analysis of clinical studies. Ultimately, the scope of clinical research extends far beyond the confines of the laboratory or the clinic. Its impact is felt in every aspect of healthcare, from the development of new treatments to the implementation of public health strategies. By answering critical questions about health and disease, clinical research serves as the foundation for advancing medical knowledge and improving the lives of patients around the world.

Key Stakeholders and Their Roles

Clinical research is a collaborative effort that involves multiple stakeholders, each playing a vital role in the process. There are researchers often referred to as Principal Investigators. Or they may be called "investigators." These are the scientists and clinicians who design and conduct the clinical trials. They formulate the research questions, develop protocols, oversee the study's execution, and analyze the data.

Sponsors are individuals or organizations, such as pharmaceutical companies, academic institutions, or government agencies, that provide the financial support necessary to conduct the study. They may also contribute to the study design and data analysis.

Sponsors play a crucial role in the clinical research process, providing the financial resources, expertise, and strategic direction required to bring new medical treatments from concept to reality. These individuals or organizations are responsible for initiating, managing, and overseeing clinical trials to ensure their successful execution. Without sponsors, the extensive costs and logistical demands of clinical research would make it challenging to advance medical innovation and improve patient care.

Sponsors come from a variety of backgrounds and sectors, each contributing unique resources and expertise to the clinical research ecosystem. Common types of sponsors include pharmaceutical and biotechnology companies, academic and research institutions, government agencies, non-profit and patient advocacy groups, medical device manufacturers, and even private investors and venture capital firms.

These organizations are the most frequent sponsors of clinical trials, investing billions of dollars annually in drug discovery and development. Their goal is to develop safe and effective treatments, secure regulatory approval, and bring new therapies to market. Pharmaceutical sponsors often fund large-scale, multi-phase trials to evaluate the safety, efficacy, and long-term effects of new drugs.

Universities, teaching hospitals, and independent research organizations often sponsor clinical trials to advance scientific knowledge and improve patient care. These sponsors typically focus on early-phase or investigator-initiated studies that explore innovative therapies, rare diseases, or novel treatment approaches.

Public health organizations like the National Institutes of Health (NIH), the Food and Drug Administration (FDA), and the European Medicines Agency (EMA) sponsor clinical research to address public health priorities. These studies may focus on emerging diseases, vaccine development, or improving health outcomes in underserved populations.

Charitable organizations and patient advocacy groups often sponsor or co-sponsor clinical trials to advance treatments for specific diseases or medical conditions. Their efforts are often directed toward rare diseases, pediatric conditions, and areas of unmet medical need that may not attract commercial investment.

Companies that develop medical devices, such as surgical instruments, diagnostic tools, and wearable technologies, sponsor clinical trials to evaluate the safety and efficacy of their products. These studies are essential for securing regulatory approval and ensuring that devices meet safety standards.

In recent years, private equity and venture capital firms have increasingly invested in clinical research through partnerships with biotech startups and emerging life sciences companies. These sponsors aim to support innovative treatments while achieving financial returns.

Sponsors are responsible for the overall conduct of clinical trials, ensuring they are performed in accordance with ethical guidelines, regulatory standards, and Good Clinical Practice (GCP). Conducting a clinical trial is an expensive and resource-intensive endeavor. Sponsors provide the necessary funding to cover trial-related costs, including site operations, participant compensation, regulatory filings, and data analysis. This financial support enables research teams to conduct robust, large-scale studies.

Sponsors often play a central role in designing the clinical trial protocol—a detailed plan that outlines the study's objectives, methodologies, patient criteria, and data collection processes. They work closely with clinical research professionals to ensure that the study is scientifically sound, ethically conducted, and capable of producing meaningful results.

Sponsors are responsible for ensuring compliance with national and international regulatory standards. This includes submitting applications for regulatory approval (e.g., Investigational New Drug (IND) application, Clinical Trial Authorization (CTA)), providing safety updates, and maintaining accurate records. Failure to comply with these regulations can result in significant delays or trial termination.

Sponsors identify and contract with clinical trial sites—hospitals, clinics, or research centers—to conduct the study. They provide the necessary resources and training to site personnel and maintain oversight to ensure adherence to the study protocol and GCP guidelines.

Sponsors oversee the collection, management, and analysis of clinical trial data. This involves ensuring data accuracy, confidentiality, and integrity. Statistical analyses are performed to evaluate the efficacy and safety of the investigational product, and these findings are critical for regulatory submissions and eventual product approval.

Protecting patient safety is a core responsibility of sponsors. They must ensure that all adverse events (AEs) and serious adverse events (SAEs) are documented and reported to regulatory authorities promptly. Sponsors may also establish independent Data Safety Monitoring Boards (DSMBs) to assess interim trial data and recommend modifications if safety concerns arise.

Sponsors are expected to maintain clear communication with investigators, regulatory agencies, and the public. This includes disseminating study results, whether positive or negative, to promote scientific transparency and inform future research. Without the support of sponsors, many groundbreaking medical innovations would not reach patients. Sponsors drive the translation of scientific discoveries into approved therapies by accelerating drug development, bridging the research gap, ensuring data integrity, and expanding patient access. Financial backing from sponsors enables clinical trials to proceed through multiple phases quickly, shortening the time between discovery and patient access. Sponsors provide funding for research areas that may lack commercial incentives, such as rare diseases and public health concerns. Rigorous sponsor oversight ensures that trial data meets the highest standards for accuracy and reliability, which is essential for regulatory approval. Sponsors facilitate the inclusion of diverse populations, helping to ensure that new treatments are safe and effective across different demographic groups.

As the clinical research landscape evolves, sponsors are adopting new approaches to enhance trial efficiency and patient engagement. Key trends shaping the future of clinical trial sponsorship include Decentralized Clinical Trials (DCTs), where sponsors are increasingly adopting remote trial designs that leverage digital health technologies to collect patient data outside traditional research sites. This reduces the burden on participants and increases accessibility. Sponsors are also considering diversity and inclusion initiatives, where they recognize the historical underrepresentation of minority populations and prioritize diversity in clinical trials. They are implementing targeted recruitment strategies to ensure trial data reflects real-world populations. Sponsors are using real-world data from electronic health records (EHRs) and patient registries to complement traditional trial data. This approach improves post-market surveillance and enhances understanding of long-term outcomes. Many sponsors are forming strategic alliances with academic institutions, patient advocacy groups, and other industry stakeholders to share expertise and resources. These collaborations foster innovation and reduce research costs.

Sponsors are the backbone of clinical research, providing the financial support, scientific expertise, and regulatory oversight necessary to bring new therapies to patients. Their work not only advances medical innovation but also ensures that clinical trials are conducted with the highest standards of ethics, safety, and scientific integrity. As the clinical research landscape continues to evolve, sponsors will remain critical players in shaping the future of healthcare and improving patient outcomes worldwide.

Contract Research Organizations (CROs) are independent organizations hired by sponsors to manage various aspects of clinical trials, including study design, data management, regulatory compliance, and site monitoring. CROs bring specialized expertise and resources, helping to ensure that trials are conducted efficiently and in compliance with regulatory standards.

Contract Research Organizations (CROs) play a pivotal role in the clinical research ecosystem, serving as independent entities hired by pharmaceutical companies, biotechnology firms, medical device manufacturers, and other sponsors to manage and execute various aspects of clinical trials. Their expertise spans the entire clinical trial lifecycle—from study design to final regulatory submission—making them invaluable partners in the development of new medical treatments. As the clinical research landscape grows increasingly complex, CROs provide the specialized knowledge, infrastructure, and operational capacity required to conduct trials efficiently, ethically, and in accordance with global regulatory standards.

CROs offer comprehensive support throughout the various phases of clinical research. Their responsibilities encompass a broad range of critical activities that ensure clinical trials are conducted successfully and in compliance with legal and ethical guidelines.

A well-structured study design is essential for generating reliable and meaningful data. CROs collaborate with sponsors to develop detailed clinical trial protocols, outlining the objectives, methodologies, patient inclusion/exclusion criteria, and endpoints. Their scientific and regulatory expertise ensures that study designs align with industry best practices while meeting the rigorous standards of regulatory bodies like the U.S. Food and Drug Administration (FDA), European Medicines Agency (EMA), and other global agencies.

Navigating the complex regulatory landscape is a significant challenge in clinical research. CROs play a crucial role in preparing and submitting documentation for regulatory approvals, including Investigational New Drug (IND) applications, Clinical Trial Applications (CTA), and New Drug Applications (NDA). They stay abreast of evolving regulations to ensure that studies comply with Good Clinical Practice (GCP), International Council for Harmonisation (ICH) guidelines, and local laws across multiple regions.

The successful execution of a clinical trial depends heavily on selecting qualified research sites and maintaining robust oversight throughout the study. CROs are responsible for identifying and onboarding trial sites that meet the study's criteria, ensuring that investigators and staff are trained on protocols, and conducting site initiation visits (SIVs). Throughout the trial, they perform interim monitoring visits (IMVs) to ensure adherence to study protocols, track patient enrollment, verify data accuracy, and ensure patient safety. Site monitoring also includes conducting close-out visits (COVs) to finalize documentation and ensure compliance once the trial concludes.

Recruiting and retaining diverse patient populations is a major challenge in clinical research. CROs leverage their networks and experience to develop patient-centric recruitment strategies that prioritize diversity and inclusion. This ensures that trial data reflects the real-world population and leads to more equitable healthcare outcomes. They also manage patient retention efforts, providing support services to minimize dropouts and maintain study integrity.

Accurate data collection and analysis are the foundation of any clinical trial. CROs implement advanced data management systems to capture, clean, and analyze clinical trial data. They ensure the integrity and security of clinical data while providing biostatistical expertise to interpret results accurately. This work is critical for demonstrating the safety and efficacy of investigational treatments.

Quality assurance (QA) is a cornerstone of clinical research. CROs establish robust quality management systems (QMS) to ensure that clinical trials meet all regulatory, ethical, and operational requirements. This includes conducting internal audits, managing corrective and preventive actions (CAPA), and mitigating risks throughout the trial process.

There are many advantages to using CROs to develop new therapies. Conducting clinical trials in-house requires substantial investments in infrastructure, staffing, and expertise. CROs streamline this process by offering established resources and operational efficiencies, reducing both the time and cost associated with drug development. Their global reach allows sponsors to conduct multi-regional trials simultaneously, accelerating timelines for regulatory approval and market entry.

CROs possess deep expertise across therapeutic areas, regulatory environments, and trial methodologies. This specialized knowledge enables them to address complex trial designs, adaptive protocols, and innovative approaches like decentralized clinical trials (DCTs) that use digital technologies to monitor patients remotely. Their ability to adopt and implement emerging technologies enhances the speed and accuracy of clinical research.

Sponsors can scale clinical operations up or down by partnering with CROs, allowing for greater flexibility in managing multiple trials across different phases. Whether a sponsor is running a small Phase I study or a large-scale, multi-country Phase III trial, CROs offer tailored support to meet specific project needs.

Many CROs operate across multiple countries, providing access to diverse patient populations and ensuring compliance with local regulatory standards. This global reach is particularly beneficial for sponsors seeking to conduct multinational trials or expand into emerging markets.

With comprehensive quality management frameworks in place, CROs help identify and mitigate risks throughout the clinical trial lifecycle. Their ability to monitor for deviations, ensure compliance, and implement CAPA measures reduces the likelihood of regulatory delays and data integrity issues.

As clinical research evolves, the role of CROs continues to expand. Emerging trends shaping the future of CROs include the use of Decentralized Clinical Trials (DCTs), which use telemedicine, remote monitoring, and wearable devices to collect patient data from home, reducing the need for in-person visits and increasing patient participation. There is also Artificial Intelligence (AI) and Big Data: leveraging AI-driven analytics to enhance patient recruitment, predict trial outcomes, and analyze vast datasets more efficiently. Another recommended approach is one that is patient-centric. This means prioritizing patient experiences by incorporating patient feedback into study design and improving trial accessibility for underrepresented populations. Lastly, there is Real-World Evidence (RWE), which collects and analyzes real-world data from electronic health records (EHRs) and patient registries to supplement clinical trial findings and improve post-market surveillance.

Contract Research Organizations are indispensable partners in the clinical research process, providing the expertise, infrastructure, and innovation needed to bring new therapies to market. Their ability to navigate regulatory complexities, manage trial logistics, and ensure data integrity allows sponsors to focus on their core mission: developing life-changing treatments. As clinical research continues to evolve, CROs will remain at the forefront of driving efficiency, ensuring compliance and advancing medical innovation.

Institutional Review Boards (IRBs) or Ethics Committees are committees that are responsible for reviewing and approving study protocols to ensure the safety and rights of participants are protected. They evaluate the ethical aspects of the study and monitor it for compliance with ethical standards. IRBs and Ethics Committees play a critical role in ensuring that clinical research is conducted ethically, safely, and with respect for the rights and welfare of participants. These committees are responsible for reviewing, approving, and monitoring research involving human subjects to ensure compliance with ethical guidelines and regulatory standards. Their work is vital to maintaining public trust in clinical research, especially in light of historical injustices that have disproportionately affected minority communities.

The establishment of IRBs and Ethics Committees was largely driven by a troubling history of unethical medical research practices. Throughout the 20th century, numerous incidents exposed the profound harm that can occur when research is conducted without adequate ethical oversight. These historical injustices primarily affected vulnerable and marginalized populations, contributing to the deep mistrust that many communities, particularly Black and underserved groups, have toward clinical research today.

Key Historical Cases of Ethical Violations

The Tuskegee Syphilis Study (1932–1972):

One of the most infamous and deeply troubling examples of unethical research in American history is the Tuskegee Syphilis Study, conducted by the U.S. Public Health Service between 1932 and 1972. In this study,

600 Black men from Macon County, Alabama, were enrolled under the guise of receiving free medical care. Of these men, 399 had syphilis and 201 did not. However, none of the participants were ever informed of their diagnosis. They were told they were being treated for "bad blood," a vague term that was commonly used at the time to describe various ailments. Most critically, they did not give their informed consent, as they were unaware of the true nature and purpose of the study.

As the study progressed, the deception deepened. Even after penicillin became the standard and effective treatment for syphilis in the 1940s, the researchers deliberately withheld this life-saving antibiotic from the participants. Instead, the men were subjected to painful and ineffective procedures, while the investigators continued to monitor the progression of the untreated disease. This deliberate denial of treatment led to immense and unnecessary suffering, as many of the men experienced severe health complications: blindness, mental impairment, and ultimately, premature death. Tragically, the consequences extended beyond the participants themselves—their spouses contracted the disease, and some of their children were born with congenital syphilis.

The study continued unchecked for 40 years until it was exposed by a whistleblower and subsequently reported in the national media in 1972. The public outrage that followed led to the termination of the study and a formal government apology decades later, in 1997, by President Bill Clinton. The Tuskegee Syphilis Study stands as a stark reminder of the exploitation and abuse faced by Black Americans within the medical system and has contributed to a longstanding mistrust of healthcare and research among communities of color. Its legacy continues to influence current ethical standards and practices, underscoring the importance of informed consent, transparency, and respect for human rights in all aspects of clinical research.

Henrietta Lacks and the HeLa Cells (1951):

Henrietta Lacks, a Black woman receiving treatment for cervical cancer at Johns Hopkins Hospital, had her cancer cells taken without her knowledge or consent. These cells, known as HeLa cells, became one of the most significant breakthroughs in medical research. While her cells revolutionized science, her family remained unaware and did not benefit financially or medically from the discoveries.

These and other cases of research abuse led to widespread public outrage and the implementation of regulatory reforms to protect human participants in research. As a result, IRBs and Ethics Committees were created to prevent such abuses from happening again.

In response to the Tuskegee Syphilis Study, the U.S. government established the National Commission for the Protection of Human Subjects of Biomedical and Behavioral Research. This commission produced the Belmont Report in 1979, which laid the ethical foundation for modern clinical research. The Belmont Report outlines three core principles that guide the work of IRBs and Ethics Committees:

- Respect for Persons: Protecting the autonomy of participants and ensuring informed consent.
- Beneficence: Minimizing harm while maximizing the potential benefits of research.
- Justice: Ensuring fair distribution of the risks and benefits of research, particularly for vulnerable populations.

These principles remain central to the work of IRBs and Ethics Committees, ensuring that research is conducted with integrity and in accordance with ethical standards. IRBs (in the United States) and Ethics Committees (in other countries) function as independent bodies that review research protocols to ensure the protection of human subjects. They assess study protocols to ensure that research is scientifically valid and ethically sound. This includes reviewing the study design, participant recruitment methods, and the informed consent process. IRBs ensure that participants are fully informed about the study's purpose, risks, benefits, and their right to withdraw at any time, which is a fundamental duty of these committees. IRBs and Ethics Committees evaluate whether the potential benefits of the research outweigh any risks to participants. They conduct regular reviews of active studies to ensure continued compliance with ethical standards. Any adverse events or deviations from the approved protocol must be reported promptly. Special protections are required for vulnerable populations, such as children, prisoners, pregnant women, and individuals with diminished capacity to consent. Modern IRBs increasingly prioritize community involvement and cultural competence, particularly when research involves underrepresented populations.

The composition of IRBs and Ethics Committees is intentionally diverse to provide a comprehensive and balanced perspective. According to federal regulations (e.g., 45 CFR 46 in the U.S.), these committees must include scientists and medical professionals, non-scientists, and community representatives. The scientists and medical professionals can be experts in clinical research, medicine, and related scientific fields who can evaluate the technical and methodological aspects of the study. The non-scientists can be individuals from non-scientific backgrounds (e.g., ethicists, social workers, educators) who provide an independent, community-based perspective and ensure research is understandable to the public. The community representatives are typically laypersons who represent the interests of the community and advocate for participant rights, especially when research involves marginalized or vulnerable groups.

To address racial bias and historical injustices, committees should reflect diverse backgrounds and lived experiences. Including members from Black and other minority communities is essential to fostering trust and ensuring cultural competency. Some committees may include legal professionals to provide guidance on compliance with local, national, and international research regulations. Diverse representation on IRBs is important for ensuring that the perspectives and concerns of marginalized communities are adequately considered. A diverse committee can help to improve cultural competence by understanding the social and cultural factors influencing participant decision-making. Diversity in the committee can also address power imbalances by ensuring that historically excluded populations are not exploited or disproportionately burdened. It can foster trust in the research process by ensuring transparency and community engagement. A diverse IRB can also help to promote equitable inclusion of diverse populations in clinical trials, addressing health disparities.

While IRBs and Ethics Committees have made significant progress, ongoing efforts are needed to strengthen ethical oversight and rebuild trust in clinical research. These efforts should include prioritizing the recruitment of individuals from underrepresented racial, ethnic, and socio-economic backgrounds. IRBs need to focus on enhancing community engagement by involving community advisory boards to co-develop research protocols that reflect community needs and values. There needs to be transparency and public reporting of research findings, including negative outcomes, to demonstrate accountability. It's also encouraging to launch educational initiatives by providing culturally sensitive education to potential participants about their rights and the value of clinical research.

By fostering ethical research practices, promoting inclusivity, and prioritizing community voices, IRBs and Ethics Committees can play a transformative role in creating a healthcare system that is equitable, transparent, and trustworthy.

Bodies such as the U.S. Food and Drug Administration (FDA) and the European Medicines Agency (EMA) regulate clinical trials, ensuring that they comply with laws and regulations. They review study protocols, monitor trial progress, and evaluate the data to approve or reject new treatments.

Participants are the individuals who volunteer to participate in clinical trials are at the heart of clinical research. Their involvement is crucial for generating the data needed to evaluate new treatments.

Ethics and Regulations Governing Clinical Trials

Ethics and regulations are the cornerstone of clinical research, ensuring that studies are conducted responsibly and participants' rights and well-being are protected. There are some important ethical principles to practice when conducting clinical trials.

There needs to be respect for persons where there is the acknowledgment of the autonomy of individuals and providing special protection to those with diminished autonomy. This principle is implemented through informed consent, ensuring that participants are fully aware of the study's nature, risks, and benefits before agreeing to take part. Beneficence is the obligation to maximize benefits and minimize harm to participants. This requires a thorough assessment of risks and benefits before initiating a study and continuous monitoring throughout the trial. Justice refers to ensuring that the benefits and burdens of research are distributed fairly. This means that no group should bear an undue burden or be unfairly excluded from the potential benefits of research.

There are several key regulations and guidelines that govern clinical research. Good Clinical Practice (GCP) is a set of internationally recognized ethical and scientific quality standards for designing, conducting, recording, and reporting clinical trials. Compliance with GCP ensures that the rights, safety, and well-being of trial participants are protected. The Declaration of Helsinki is a set of ethical principles developed by the World Medical Association to guide medical researchers in conducting human research. It emphasizes the importance of informed consent and the necessity of balancing risks and benefits. The Belmont Report is a key document in the history of clinical research ethics in the United States, outlining the ethical principles and guidelines for research involving human subjects, including respect for persons, beneficence, and justice. 21 CFR Part 11 is a regulation by the FDA that sets forth the criteria under which electronic records and electronic signatures are considered trustworthy, reliable, and equivalent to paper records.

Overview of the Drug Development Process

The drug development process is a long, complex journey that can typically span 10–15 years and involves multiple stages. First, there is discovery and preclinical research. This initial stage involves identifying potential drug candidates and testing them in the lab, as well as in animal models to evaluate their safety and biological activity. The goal is to identify promising compounds that warrant further investigation.

An Investigational New Drug (IND) Application needs to be submitted before testing a new drug in humans, and researchers must submit an IND application to regulatory authorities. The IND includes data from preclinical studies, the proposed clinical trial protocol, and information about the drug's composition and manufacturing.

Once the previous has passed, an investigator can move forward with Clinical Trials Phases I–IV. Phase I trials involve a small number of healthy volunteers (or patients) and focus on evaluating the drug's safety, dosage, and pharmacokinetics. Phase II trials involve a larger group of patients and aim to assess the drug's efficacy and further evaluate its safety. Phase III trials are large-scale trials involving hundreds or thousands of patients. They aim to confirm the drug's efficacy, monitor side effects, and compare it to existing treatments. Phase IV refers to post-marketing studies that are conducted after the drug has been approved and marketed. They aim to gather additional information about the drug's long-term safety, efficacy, and optimal use.

If the results from clinical trials are positive, the sponsor submits a New Drug Application (NDA) to regulatory authorities, requesting approval to market the drug. The NDA includes data from all preclinical and clinical studies, information about the drug's manufacturing process, and proposed labeling. Regulatory authorities review the NDA to ensure that the drug is safe, effective, and manufactured to high-quality standards. This review process can take several months to years, depending on the complexity of the drug and the data submitted.

Once a drug is approved and marketed, ongoing surveillance is conducted to monitor its safety and efficacy in the general population. This phase is crucial for detecting rare or long-term adverse effects that may not have been apparent in clinical trials.

CHAPTER 3

Essential Skills for Clinical Researchers

In the intricate world of clinical research, developing a strong skill set is crucial for navigating the complexities of this field. These skills not only set you apart but also ensure the success and integrity of the studies you conduct. In this chapter, we'll explore the essential skills every clinical researcher should master, including protocol design and development, adherence to Good Clinical Practice (GCP) guidelines, effective data collection and management, and strategies for patient recruitment and retention.

The clinical trial protocol is the blueprint for any study, outlining every detail from objectives and design to methodology and statistical considerations. A well-crafted protocol is the foundation of a scientifically sound and ethically responsible study, ensuring that the research is feasible and that all aspects are thoroughly planned. The protocol must clearly define the study's primary and secondary objectives, ensuring that the research questions are specific and measurable. The study design must be carefully chosen to align with these objectives, whether it's a randomized controlled trial, observational study, or another type of research. Critical to the protocol is the selection of the study population, with inclusion and exclusion criteria that precisely identify who will participate in the study, ensuring that the results are applicable to the target population.

A detailed description of the interventions being tested, including dosages, methods of administration, and duration, is also essential. The protocol must also specify the primary and secondary endpoints, which are the key outcomes that will be measured to determine the study's success. Equally important is the statistical plan, which outlines how the data will be analyzed, including sample size calculations and any interim analyses.

Safety monitoring procedures are integral to the protocol, ensuring that adverse events are tracked and reported in a timely manner, safeguarding the well-being of participants. Ethical considerations, including the informed consent process and the protection of participant confidentiality, must also be rigorously addressed and reviewed by an Institutional Review Board (IRB) or Ethics Committee.

The development of a clinical trial protocol involves several key steps: conducting a thorough literature review to identify gaps in current knowledge, developing a clear research question and hypothesis, drafting the protocol with all necessary components, and submitting it to stakeholders for review and approval. Once approved, the protocol becomes the guiding document for the study, with the research team trained on its contents to ensure consistent implementation.

Good Clinical Practice (GCP) guidelines are the ethical and scientific standards that govern the design, conduct, recording, and reporting of clinical trials. Compliance with GCP ensures that the rights, safety, and well-being of trial participants are protected and that the data generated is credible and reliable. GCP is grounded in ethical principles that originate from the Declaration of Helsinki, emphasizing the importance of conducting trials with integrity and respect for participants. One of the core tenets of GCP is protocol compliance, ensuring that trials are scientifically sound and that all study procedures are followed as outlined in the protocol. Informed consent is another critical component, requiring that participants are fully informed about the study and voluntarily agree to participate.

Confidentiality is paramount under GCP, with strict guidelines to protect the identities of participants and the privacy of their data. Data quality is also emphasized, with requirements for accurate, consistent, and verifiable data collection, handling, and storage. Safety reporting is another key aspect, with adverse events needing to be promptly reported to relevant authorities according to regulatory requirements. Implementing GCP in clinical trials involves several steps, starting with ensuring that all study personnel are trained in GCP principles and procedures. Comprehensive documentation is essential, from case report forms (CRFs) and informed consent forms to adverse event reports. Regular monitoring visits are conducted to ensure compliance with the protocol and GCP guidelines, and audits by sponsors, regulatory authorities, or independent auditors may be conducted to verify adherence to these standards.

Accurate and reliable data collection and management are critical to the success of any clinical trial. The integrity of a study's findings and its eventual regulatory approval hinge on the quality of the data collected. Data collection begins with the design of Case Report Forms (CRFs), which are standardized forms used to collect data from each study participant. These forms should be clear, concise, and tailored to the study's objectives, ensuring that all relevant data is captured. Increasingly, clinical trials use Electronic Data Capture (EDC) systems, which allow for data to be entered, managed, and stored electronically. These systems enhance data accuracy, reduce the risk of errors, and facilitate real-time data monitoring.

Source documents, such as medical records and laboratory reports, are used to verify the accuracy and completeness of the data recorded in the

CRFs. The data management process includes data entry, where information from CRFs is accurately and promptly entered into the EDC system. Data cleaning is a critical step, involving the review of data for inconsistencies, errors, and missing values, with any issues resolved through data queries. Once the data has been cleaned, the database is locked to prevent further changes, allowing the data to be analyzed according to the statistical plan outlined in the protocol.

Recruiting and retaining participants in clinical trials is one of the most challenging aspects of clinical research, yet it is essential for the timely completion of studies and the validity of the results. Effective recruitment strategies begin with clearly defining the eligibility criteria, including inclusion and exclusion criteria that help identify suitable participants. Outreach methods, such as advertisements, social media campaigns, and community engagement, are used to reach potential participants. Building partnerships with healthcare providers, patient advocacy groups, and community organizations can also help identify and recruit participants. Offering incentives, such as compensation for time and travel, can encourage participation and make it easier for individuals to commit to their studies.

Retention strategies are equally important for ensuring that participants remain engaged and complete the study. Regular communication with participants helps to keep them informed and involved, reducing the likelihood of dropouts. Providing support services, such as transportation assistance and flexible scheduling, can help accommodate participants' needs and reduce barriers to continued participation. Implementing follow-up procedures to monitor participants' progress and address any concerns promptly is also crucial. Gathering feedback from participants can help identify and address any issues that may affect retention, improving the overall participant experience and the success of the study.

By mastering these essential skills, protocol design and development, adherence to GCP guidelines, data collection and management, and patient recruitment and retention strategies, clinical researchers can navigate the complexities of their field with confidence and contribute to the advancement of medical knowledge and patient care.

CHAPTER 4

Conducting Successful Clinical Trials

xecuting clinical trials efficiently and effectively is essential for achieving milestones. This chapter addresses phase-specific trial management (Phase I to IV), site selection and management, monitoring and quality assurance, and adverse event reporting and safety monitoring.

Phase I of clinical trials marks the first stage where a new drug is tested in humans. The primary objective of this phase is to assess the safety, tolerability, pharmacokinetics, and pharmacodynamics of the drug. Typically, this phase involves a small group of participants, often ranging from 20 to 100 individuals. These participants are usually healthy volunteers, though in some cases, patients with the condition being targeted by the drug may be recruited, particularly when the drug is expected to have significant side effects. The main goal of Phase I trials is to establish the safety profile of the drug. Researchers are primarily concerned with understanding how the drug behaves in the human body—how it is absorbed, distributed, metabolized, and excreted (pharmacokinetics), as well as how it affects the body (pharmacodynamics). This phase is critical for determining the appropriate dosage levels that can be safely administered to participants. It also helps in identifying any potential side effects or adverse reactions at various dosage levels.

One of the first steps in a Phase I trial is participant recruitment. Depending on the nature of the drug, the trial may focus on healthy volunteers or a specific patient population that could benefit from the treatment. The selection criteria are stringent, ensuring that the participants are suitable for the study and minimizing any risk of harm. The dosing strategy in Phase I trials is carefully planned. Researchers start with a low dose, gradually increasing it to determine the maximum tolerated dose (MTD). This approach, often referred to as dose-escalation, is designed to find the highest dose that can be administered without causing unacceptable side effects. This process is meticulously monitored, with participants being observed closely for any signs of adverse events (AEs) or side effects.

Safety monitoring is a continuous process throughout the trial. Researchers track all AEs, regardless of their severity or whether they are expected. This includes monitoring vital signs, laboratory results, and other clinical parameters that could indicate how the drug is affecting the participants. Any serious adverse events (SAEs) are promptly reported to regulatory authorities and ethics committees to determine whether the trial can safely continue.

Data collection during Phase I is extensive and focuses on the pharmacokinetic and pharmacodynamic properties of the drug. Researchers collect data on how the drug is absorbed into the bloodstream, how it is distributed throughout the body, how it is metabolized by the liver or other organs, and how it is ultimately excreted. This data is crucial for understanding the drug's behavior in the human body and helps guide the dosing strategies for subsequent phases of clinical trials.

Conducting a Phase I trial comes with several challenges, the foremost being ensuring participant safety. Since this is the first time the drug is being tested in humans, there is a level of uncertainty about how participants will respond, and researchers must be prepared to address any unexpected reactions promptly. Another significant challenge is managing the complex pharmacokinetic analyses required in this phase. Understanding the intricate processes of how a drug is absorbed, metabolized, and excreted requires sophisticated techniques and experienced researchers. These analyses are essential for determining the drug's safety profile and for planning the dosage regimens for future phases of clinical testing. Phase I trials are a crucial step in the drug development process, providing the first insights into the drug's safety and how it interacts with the human body. The data collected during this phase lays the groundwork for further studies, helping to ensure that the drug can be safely tested in larger groups of participants in subsequent trial phases.

Phase II of clinical trials looks at safety and efficacy, and it is a critical stage in the drug development process, where the focus shifts from initial safety assessments to evaluating the drug's efficacy while continuing to monitor its safety. This phase involves a larger group of participants, typically ranging from 100 to 300 patients who have the condition that the drug is intended to treat. The objective of Phase II trials is to determine whether the drug has the desired therapeutic effect and to further refine the understanding of its safety profile.

The primary objective of Phase II is to evaluate the drug's efficacy in a patient population, determining whether it effectively treats the targeted condition. In addition, researchers continue to monitor the drug's safety, identifying any adverse effects that may not have been evident in the smaller Phase I trials. This phase also helps establish the optimal dose that provides the maximum therapeutic benefit with the fewest side effects.

Phase II trials are often designed as randomized, controlled studies, which are the gold standard for clinical research. In these trials, patients are randomly assigned to receive either the experimental drug, a placebo, or a standard treatment (if one exists). This study design allows researchers to compare the new drug's efficacy directly against a control, providing robust data on how well the drug works relative to other treatments.

Selecting the appropriate endpoints is a crucial part of Phase II trial design. Endpoints are the specific outcomes that researchers measure to determine the drug's efficacy. Primary endpoints are typically related to the main therapeutic effect of the drug, such as symptom improvement or disease progression. Secondary endpoints may include additional measures of efficacy, such as quality of life, as well as safety outcomes, like the incidence of side effects. Patient monitoring continues to be a significant focus in Phase II, with regular assessments to track any adverse events (AEs) or side effects that arise. The safety of participants remains paramount, and any new safety concerns that emerge during this phase can influence the design of future studies or, in some cases, halt the development of the drug altogether.

Data analysis in Phase II involves assessing the drug's efficacy based on the pre-defined endpoints. Researchers also examine the data for any dose-response relationships, which help determine the optimal dose for future studies. This analysis is critical for understanding how different doses affect both the efficacy and safety of the drug, guiding dosing decisions in subsequent phases.

One of the main challenges in Phase II is balancing the need to gather robust efficacy data with the imperative to ensure patient safety. As the trial involves more patients and explores higher or varied doses, the potential for side effects increases, requiring careful monitoring and management. Researchers must be vigilant in detecting any adverse trends early to protect participants and maintain the integrity of the study. Managing a larger and more diverse patient population also presents challenges. Unlike the relatively homogeneous groups often seen in Phase I, Phase II trials include patients with varying degrees of disease severity, co-morbidities, and backgrounds. This diversity is crucial for understanding how the drug performs in the real world, but it also adds complexity to the study, requiring more sophisticated statistical analyses and careful interpretation of the results. Phase II is a pivotal stage in clinical research that provides essential data on the drug's efficacy and further refines its safety profile. The outcomes of Phase II trials determine whether a drug is promising enough to proceed to the larger, more definitive Phase III trials, where its effectiveness will be tested in an even broader population.

Phase III clinical trials represent a crucial stage in the drug development process, where the primary goal is to confirm the drug's efficacy and further monitor its safety in a much larger and more diverse patient population. This phase is often the most extensive and resource-intensive part of clinical research, as it involves a rigorous evaluation of the drug's performance across various sites and patient demographics. The results from Phase III trials are pivotal in determining whether a drug can be approved for widespread use. The main objective of Phase III trials is to confirm the therapeutic efficacy of the drug observed in earlier phases and to ensure that it is safe for use in a broader population. These trials typically involve thousands of participants, providing a robust dataset that can offer statistically significant evidence of the drug's benefits. Additionally, Phase III trials continue to monitor side effects and other safety concerns, ensuring that any risks associated with the drug are well-understood before it is considered for regulatory approval.

The design of Phase III trials is typically large-scale and multicenter, often involving numerous clinical sites across different geographical locations. This approach ensures that the drug's efficacy and safety are tested in a diverse patient population, which is essential for understanding how the drug will perform in real-world settings. These trials are designed to reflect the conditions under which the drug will be used once it is approved, providing critical insights into its generalizability and effectiveness. Randomization and blinding are fundamental components of Phase III trials to minimize bias and ensure the reliability of the results. Participants are randomly assigned to receive either the experimental drug, a placebo, or an existing standard treatment, depending on the trial's design. Blinding—where neither the participants nor the researchers know who is receiving the treatment—further reduces the potential for bias, ensuring that the observed effects are due to the drug itself and not influenced by placebo effects or researchers' expectations. Data collection in Phase III is extensive and methodical, focusing on both efficacy and safety outcomes. Researchers gather detailed data on how well the drug works in treating the condition, as well as any side effects or adverse events that occur during the trial. This data is critical for understanding the drug's risk-benefit profile and for preparing the documentation required for regulatory submissions.

As Phase III trials near completion, preparations for regulatory submissions become a key focus. This phase culminates in the preparation of a New Drug Application (NDA) or a Biologics License Application (BLA), depending on the nature of the drug. These submissions include all the data collected throughout the clinical trials, along with detailed analyses and justifications for why the drug should be approved for public use. The regulatory review process is rigorous, and the quality and completeness of the Phase III data are crucial for gaining approval.

Conducting Phase III trials presents several significant challenges, the foremost being the coordination of multiple sites and large patient cohorts. Managing a trial across numerous locations requires meticulous planning and coordination to ensure consistency in how the trial is conducted and data is collected. Variations in site performance, patient recruitment, and adherence to protocols can all impact the trial's outcomes, so maintaining oversight and quality control is essential. Ensuring data integrity and compliance with regulatory standards is another major challenge. The large volume of data collected during Phase III trials must be accurate, complete, and verifiable. Regulatory agencies scrutinize this data closely, so any discrepancies or errors can delay or jeopardize the drug's approval. Researchers must implement robust data management practices, including regular monitoring, audits, and validation processes, to ensure that the data meets the required standards. Phase III trials are a critical step in confirming a drug's efficacy and safety on a large scale. The outcomes of these trials are instrumental in determining whether a drug will receive regulatory approval and become available for widespread use. The success of a Phase III trial depends on careful planning, rigorous execution, and meticulous data management, all aimed at demonstrating that the drug can effectively and safely meet the needs of patients in the real world.

Phase IV, also known as post-marketing surveillance, is a crucial stage in the lifecycle of a drug that begins after it has received regulatory approval and is available for use in the general population. While the earlier phases of clinical trials focus on establishing the safety and efficacy of a drug in controlled environments, Phase IV shifts the focus to monitoring its performance in real-world settings over an extended period. This phase is essential for understanding the drug's long-term effects, its impact on diverse patient populations, and for identifying any rare or delayed adverse events (AEs) that may not have been evident during the pre-approval trials. The primary objective of Phase IV is to monitor the long-term safety and effectiveness of the drug in a broad, real-world population. This phase allows for the observation of the drug's effects over a more extended period and in a much larger and more diverse group of patients than those typically included in pre-approval clinical trials. By continuing to assess the drug after it has entered the market, researchers and regulatory bodies can ensure that it remains safe and effective for public use.

One of the central activities in Phase IV is the collection of real-world evidence (RWE), which involves gathering data on the drug's performance in everyday clinical practice. Unlike the controlled environments of clinical trials, real-world settings can reveal how the drug behaves in a wider array of patients, including those with varying health conditions, ages, and co-medications. This data is critical for understanding how the drug works in a more representative patient population and can provide insights that were not apparent in the earlier phases of development.

Safety monitoring remains a key priority in Phase IV, with ongoing surveillance to identify any rare or long-term adverse effects that may emerge as the drug is used by more people over time. Some side effects may only become apparent after prolonged use or in specific subgroups of patients, making continued vigilance essential. Pharmacovigilance systems are often employed to track and analyze reports of adverse events, allowing for a rapid response if any new safety concerns arise. The effectiveness of the drug is also reassessed during Phase IV, with researchers evaluating how well it performs in broader patient populations compared to the controlled environments of earlier trials. This can involve comparing the drug's real-world outcomes with those predicted by clinical trial data, as well as studying its impact on different subsets of patients, such as those with comorbidities or who are taking other medications.

Regulatory reporting is another critical aspect of Phase IV. The findings from post-marketing surveillance must be regularly reported to regulatory authorities, such as the FDA or EMA, to ensure that any new information about the drug's safety and effectiveness is communicated promptly. This reporting can lead to updates in the drug's labeling, new usage recommendations, or, in some cases, withdrawal from the market if significant safety issues are identified.

Phase IV presents several challenges, particularly in identifying and responding to rare or long-term adverse events. As the drug is used by a much larger and more diverse population, the likelihood of encountering rare side effects increases. Detecting these events requires robust data collection systems and careful analysis to distinguish between drug-related effects and those due to other factors. Managing large-scale data collection from diverse sources is another significant challenge in Phase IV. Data is often gathered from various settings, including hospitals, outpatient clinics, and pharmacies, and may come from different countries and healthcare systems. Ensuring the consistency, accuracy, and completeness of this data is critical for making reliable assessments about the drug's ongoing safety and effectiveness. Phase IV post-marketing surveillance is a vital component of drug development that extends beyond the initial approval process. It provides ongoing oversight of the drug's performance in the real world, helping to ensure that it continues to be safe and effective for all patients. The success of Phase IV relies on comprehensive data collection, rigorous safety monitoring, and close collaboration with regulatory authorities to protect public health.

Site Selection and Management

Selecting and managing clinical trial sites are among the most critical aspects of ensuring the success of a clinical trial. The choice of site can significantly influence the quality of data collected, the speed at which the trial progresses, and overall compliance with regulatory requirements. Effective site management is essential for maintaining the integrity of the trial, ensuring that it is conducted efficiently, and that all activities align with the study protocol and regulatory standards. The process of site selection begins with identifying potential sites that have the appropriate infrastructure, experience, and patient population necessary to conduct the trial. This involves evaluating each site's track record in conducting similar trials, their recruitment capabilities, and their ability to comply with Good Clinical Practice (GCP) guidelines. Sites with experienced investigators, well-trained staff, and access to the target patient population are often preferred, as these factors can reduce the risk of delays and ensure high-quality data collection. The geographical location of the site is also a consideration, as it can impact patient recruitment and retention, as well as the logistical aspects of trial management.

Once sites are selected, effective management becomes crucial to the trial's success. This includes establishing clear lines of communication between the sponsor, the Contract Research Organization (CRO), and the site personnel. Regular monitoring visits are conducted to ensure that the site adheres to the study protocol, follows regulatory requirements, and maintains accurate and complete documentation. These visits also help identify and resolve any issues early in the trial process, minimizing the risk of protocol deviations or data discrepancies. Training and support for site staff are key components of site management. Providing comprehensive training on the study protocol, data collection procedures, and safety monitoring requirements ensures that the site staff are fully prepared to conduct the trial. This training should be ongoing, with updates provided as the trial progresses or as new information becomes available.

Another important aspect of site management is patient recruitment and retention. Sites need to be supported in their efforts to recruit eligible participants and to keep them engaged throughout the trial. This may involve implementing strategies for patient outreach, education, and follow-up, as well as addressing any barriers to participation, such as transportation or scheduling challenges.

Managing clinical trial sites is not without challenges. Differences in experience levels among sites, varying interpretations of the protocol, and logistical issues can all impact the smooth operation of a trial. Additionally, sites may face difficulties in recruiting the target number of participants, especially if the trial involves a rare disease or a specific patient population. To mitigate these challenges, sponsors and CROs must work closely with sites to provide the necessary resources and support, monitor progress closely, and address issues proactively. Site selection and management are pivotal to the successful execution of a clinical trial. By carefully choosing the right sites and providing robust management and support, sponsors can ensure that trials are conducted efficiently, compliantly, and yield reliable results. Effective site management ultimately contributes to the overall success of the trial, ensuring that it meets its objectives and provides valuable data for the development of new therapies.

Selecting the right site for a clinical trial is a fundamental step that can greatly influence the success and efficiency of the study. The site selection process involves evaluating several key criteria to ensure that the chosen sites are well-equipped to conduct the trial according to protocol and regulatory standards. A primary criterion for site selection is the site's experience and expertise, particularly in conducting similar trials. It is essential to assess the site's history with similar studies, as this experience often correlates with their ability to handle the complexities of the trial effectively. Sites with a proven track record in managing similar research will typically have established procedures, knowledgeable staff, and a deep understanding of the study's requirements. Equally important is the qualification of the investigators leading the trial. Experienced principal investigators (PIs) who have successfully conducted trials in the past bring invaluable knowledge and skills, enhancing the likelihood of the study being conducted smoothly and yielding high-quality data. Evaluating the credentials, training, and previous performance of both the PI and the site's research staff helps ensure that the site has the necessary expertise to conduct the trial effectively.

Another critical criterion is the site's access to the required patient population. The ability of a site to recruit and retain participants who meet the study's inclusion criteria is crucial for the trial's success. This involves assessing the site's patient demographics, existing patient database, and recruitment strategies. Sites that are well-established in the community or those affiliated with large healthcare networks often have better access to a diverse pool of potential participants. It is also beneficial to evaluate the site's previous success in recruiting patients for similar studies, as this can provide insight into their ability to meet recruitment targets. Ensuring that the site can reach and engage the target population is key to achieving timely enrollment and maintaining the study's overall timeline.

The site's facilities and equipment play a vital role in the successful conduct of a clinical trial. It is important to assess whether the site has the necessary infrastructure to support the study, including appropriate laboratory space, clinical examination rooms, and equipment for data collection and analysis. The quality and condition of the equipment used in the study are also critical, as outdated or malfunctioning equipment can compromise data integrity and participant safety. Sites should be equipped to handle the specific requirements of the trial, such as specialized imaging equipment or laboratory testing facilities. A site with modern, well-maintained facilities and equipment will be better positioned to conduct the trial efficiently and effectively.

Ensuring regulatory compliance is another essential criterion in site selection. The site must adhere to local, national, and international regulatory requirements, including Good Clinical Practice (GCP) guidelines. This involves evaluating the site's history with regulatory audits and inspections, ensuring that they have a track record of compliance and that any previous issues have been adequately addressed. Sites should also have established procedures for managing regulatory documentation, reporting adverse events, and maintaining patient confidentiality. A site with a strong compliance history is less likely to encounter regulatory issues that could delay or jeopardize the trial. Selecting a clinical trial site involves a comprehensive evaluation of several critical factors. The site's experience and expertise, access to the required patient population, facilities and equipment, and regulatory compliance are all pivotal in ensuring that the trial is conducted successfully. By carefully assessing these criteria, sponsors and CROs can choose sites that are well-prepared to meet the study's demands, ultimately contributing to the trial's overall success and the reliability of its outcomes.

Effective site management is pivotal to the success of a clinical trial, ensuring that it runs smoothly and complies with all relevant protocols and regulatory requirements. This chapter explores key strategies for managing clinical trial sites, focusing on training and support, communication, monitoring visits, and performance metrics, all of which are crucial for maintaining the integrity and quality of the trial.

One of the cornerstones of successful site management is providing comprehensive training and ongoing support to site staff. At the outset of the trial, it is essential to offer detailed training sessions to educate the site staff about the study protocol, procedures, and regulatory requirements. This training ensures that all team members understand their roles and responsibilities and are equipped to handle the specific demands of the trial. Additionally, ongoing support is crucial throughout the trial's duration. This support may include regular refresher courses, access to resources and guidance from experts, and assistance with troubleshooting any issues that arise. By investing in thorough training and continuous support, sponsors can help site staff perform their duties effectively and maintain high standards of quality and compliance.

Maintaining regular and effective communication with site staff is another key strategy for successful site management. Regular interactions help to build strong working relationships, ensure that all parties are aligned with the study's goals, and address any issues promptly. Scheduled meetings, status updates, and open lines of communication enable the sponsor and site staff to discuss progress, resolve any challenges, and provide feedback. This proactive approach to communication helps to identify potential problems early and facilitates swift resolution, minimizing disruptions to the trial and ensuring that the study remains on track.

Regular monitoring visits are critical to ensuring that the trial is conducted in compliance with the study protocol and Good Clinical Practice (GCP) guidelines. These visits involve on-site inspections by clinical research associates (CRAs) or monitors who review the trial's progress, verify data accuracy, and ensure adherence to regulatory standards. During these visits, monitors assess various aspects of the trial, including participant recruitment, data collection procedures, and the handling of adverse events. Monitoring visits also provide an opportunity to identify any deviations from the protocol and address them before they impact the trial's outcomes. By conducting these visits systematically and consistently, sponsors can ensure that the trial is conducted with high integrity and that any issues are promptly resolved.

Tracking site performance using key metrics is essential for evaluating the trial's progress and identifying areas for improvement. Performance metrics typically include recruitment rates, data quality, and adherence to timelines. Monitoring recruitment rates helps assess whether the site is meeting its enrollment targets and can highlight any barriers to participant recruitment. Data quality metrics involve reviewing the accuracy, completeness, and timeliness of data submissions, ensuring that the data collected is reliable and valid. Adherence to timelines is another important metric, as it reflects the site's ability to complete study milestones and tasks according to the established schedule. By regularly reviewing these performance metrics, sponsors can gain insights into site performance, address any issues proactively, and make data-driven decisions to enhance the trial's overall success.

Monitoring and Quality Assurance

Monitoring and quality assurance are integral to ensuring the integrity of clinical trials and the reliability of the data generated. Effective monitoring involves not only routine site visits and compliance checks but also a comprehensive quality assurance program that includes standard operating procedures (SOPs), regular audits, and corrective actions. Quality assurance activities are designed to uphold the highest standards of data accuracy, participant safety, and regulatory compliance. By implementing robust monitoring and quality assurance practices, sponsors can maintain the credibility of the trial, ensure adherence to regulatory requirements, and ultimately support the successful completion of the study.

Effective site management involves a multifaceted approach that includes thorough training and support, consistent communication, regular monitoring visits, and performance tracking. By employing these strategies, sponsors can ensure that clinical trials are conducted efficiently, compliantly, and with the highest standards of quality, ultimately contributing to the success of the research and the integrity of its outcomes.

Site Initiation Visits (SIVs) are a critical step in the clinical trial process, conducted to ensure that trial sites are fully prepared to commence the study. During an SIV, the sponsor or Contract Research Organization (CRO) representatives visit the site to review and confirm that all necessary preparations are in place. This includes verifying that site personnel are adequately trained on the study protocol, understanding the procedures and requirements, and have access to the required resources and facilities. Additionally, the SIV serves as an opportunity to review and finalize regulatory documents, ensure that the site is compliant with Good Clinical Practice (GCP) guidelines, and address any logistical or operational issues before the trial begins. Ensuring that all these elements are in place helps to set a solid foundation for the trial and minimizes the risk of issues arising once the study is underway.

Interim Monitoring Visits (IMVs) are conducted regularly throughout the course of a clinical trial to assess the ongoing performance and compliance of the site. These visits involve a detailed review of the data collected, verification of adherence to the study protocol, and evaluation of site operations. The primary goals of IMVs are to ensure that data is being recorded accurately, to identify and address any issues or discrepancies early, and to provide support and guidance to site staff. During IMVs, monitors check for protocol deviations, ensure that informed consent procedures are being followed, and assess the overall conduct of the trial. Addressing issues promptly during these visits helps to maintain the integrity of the trial and ensures that the study remains on track.

Close-Out Visits (COVs) are conducted at the conclusion of a clinical trial to ensure that all aspects of the study are completed and that the site is ready for closure. The main objectives of a COV are to verify that all data has been collected, recorded, and submitted appropriately and to ensure that all regulatory and study-specific requirements have been met. During a COV, the monitor reviews the final data, checks for any missing or incomplete records, and ensures that all documentation is in order. Additionally, the COV provides an opportunity to address any outstanding issues, complete final regulatory submissions, and ensure that the site is properly closed out according to protocol. This thorough review and finalization process is essential for ensuring that the trial's data is complete, accurate, and reliable.

Standard Operating Procedures (SOPs) are essential for maintaining consistency and quality in clinical trials. SOPs outline the standardized processes and procedures that must be followed for all trial activities, from protocol implementation to data management and reporting. Developing and adhering to SOPs ensures that all trial activities are conducted in a systematic and compliant manner, reducing the risk of errors and inconsistencies. SOPs provide clear guidelines for site staff, monitors, and other stakeholders, ensuring that everyone involved in the trial understands their roles and responsibilities and follows the same procedures. Regular review and updating of SOPs are also crucial to incorporate new regulatory requirements, technological advancements, or improvements in best practices.

Audits are a key component of quality assurance in clinical trials, serving to verify compliance with SOPs, Good Clinical Practice (GCP), and regulatory requirements. Internal audits are conducted by the sponsor or CRO to assess the trial's adherence to established procedures and identify any areas for improvement. External audits, performed by regulatory authorities or independent auditors, provide an objective evaluation of the trial's compliance and overall quality. Both types of audits involve a thorough review of documentation, processes, and data to ensure that the trial is conducted ethically and in accordance with all applicable standards. The findings from audits are used to address any issues, implement corrective actions, and enhance the overall quality and integrity of the trial.

Corrective and Preventive Actions (CAPA) are critical for addressing and resolving issues identified during monitoring, audits, or other quality assurance activities. CAPA involves implementing corrective actions to address specific problems or deviations from the protocol and preventive actions to prevent similar issues from recurring in the future. The CAPA process includes identifying the root causes of problems, developing and implementing action plans, and monitoring the effectiveness of these actions. By systematically addressing issues and implementing improvements, CAPA helps to enhance the overall quality of the trial, ensure compliance with regulatory requirements, and protect participant safety.

Adverse Event Reporting and Safety Monitoring

Effective adverse event reporting and safety monitoring are fundamental to protecting participants and ensuring the reliability of clinical trial data. Adverse events (AEs) are any undesirable experiences or outcomes that occur in participants during the trial, regardless of whether they are related to the study drug or intervention. Prompt and accurate reporting of AEs is essential for assessing the safety profile of the drug and ensuring that any potential risks are managed appropriately. Safety monitoring involves continuous evaluation of AEs, including their severity, frequency, and potential causal relationship with the study intervention. Regular safety reviews help to identify any emerging safety concerns, ensure that appropriate actions are taken to mitigate risks, and provide timely updates to regulatory authorities and stakeholders. Effective safety monitoring and reporting contribute to the ethical conduct of the trial and support the development of safe and effective therapies.

The identification and documentation of adverse events (AEs) and serious adverse events (SAEs) are fundamental aspects of clinical trial safety monitoring. AEs are any undesirable experiences or symptoms that occur in participants during the trial, regardless of whether they are related to the study intervention. SAEs are AEs that result in significant outcomes, such as death, life-threatening conditions, hospitalization, or significant disability. It is essential for clinical trial sites to have robust procedures in place to ensure that all AEs and SAEs are promptly identified and documented. This involves thorough monitoring of participants throughout the study, including regular assessments and evaluations. Participants should be encouraged to report any new or worsening symptoms, and site staff must be trained to recognize and document these events accurately. Detailed documentation includes recording the nature of the event, its onset and duration, and any actions taken in response. Accurate identification and documentation are crucial for maintaining participant safety and ensuring that the trial data is reliable.

Once identified, adverse events must be classified based on their severity, causality, and outcome to assess their impact on participant safety and the trial's integrity. Severity refers to the intensity of the adverse event, ranging from mild to severe. Causality involves evaluating whether the adverse event is related to the study intervention, including determining if there is a likely, possible, or unlikely connection between the event and the intervention. The outcome of the adverse event is also categorized, which includes whether the event resolved, persisted, or led to a change in the participant's condition. This classification process helps in understanding the risk profile of the study intervention and informs decisions about the trial's continuation, modification, or termination. It also aids in the interpretation of safety data and the development of risk management strategies.

Reporting adverse events is a critical component of regulatory compliance and participant safety. Adverse events and serious adverse events must be reported to the sponsor, Institutional Review Board (IRB) or ethics committee, and regulatory authorities in a timely manner as stipulated by regulatory requirements. The sponsor is responsible for overseeing the overall safety of the trial and must be informed of all AEs and SAEs to ensure appropriate responses and safety measures are implemented. The IRB or ethics committee reviews these reports to ensure that participant safety is being maintained and that the study complies with ethical standards. Regulatory authorities, such as the FDA or EMA, require detailed reports to monitor the safety profile of the investigational drug or intervention and make informed decisions about its approval and use. Accurate and timely reporting helps to ensure that safety concerns are addressed promptly and contributes to the overall credibility and ethical conduct of the clinical trial.

Safety Monitoring Activities

Data Safety Monitoring Boards (DSMBs) play a crucial role in ensuring the safety and integrity of clinical trials by providing independent oversight and making informed recommendations based on safety data. DSMBs are typically composed of experts in clinical research, biostatistics, and relevant medical specialties who review trial data periodically to assess the risk-benefit profile of the study intervention. Their primary responsibility is to evaluate adverse events, serious adverse events, and other safety concerns that arise during the trial. DSMBs have the authority to recommend modifications to the trial protocol, such as adjusting dosages, altering study endpoints, or implementing additional safety measures. In some cases, they may even advise discontinuation of the trial if the risks are deemed to outweigh the benefits. This independent review process is essential for maintaining the ethical standards of clinical research and ensuring that participant safety is prioritized throughout the study.

Preparing and submitting safety reports is a critical component of regulatory compliance and transparency in clinical trials. Safety reports include periodic safety update reports (PSURs) and development safety update reports (DSURs), which provide comprehensive summaries of the safety data collected during the trial. PSURs are submitted at regular intervals and provide an overview of the safety profile of the investigational drug, including new adverse events, changes in the incidence or severity of known adverse events, and any emerging safety concerns. DSURs are typically prepared annually and focus on the safety data from ongoing clinical trials, offering a detailed analysis of the safety profile and any actions taken in response to identified risks. These reports are submitted to regulatory authorities, such as the FDA or EMA, to ensure that they are informed about the safety of the study intervention and can make decisions regarding its continued development and potential approval. Accurate and timely submission of these reports is vital for maintaining regulatory compliance and protecting participant safety.

Implementing effective risk management plans is essential for identifying, assessing, and mitigating potential safety risks throughout the clinical trial process. Risk management involves a proactive approach to identifying potential hazards and developing strategies to manage them effectively. This includes conducting risk assessments to evaluate the likelihood and impact of various risks, such as adverse events, protocol deviations, or data integrity issues. Based on these assessments, risk management plans are developed to outline specific actions and interventions to mitigate identified risks. These plans may include enhanced monitoring procedures, additional training for site staff, or adjustments to the study protocol. Ongoing risk management is crucial for adapting to new information and emerging safety concerns during the trial. By continuously assessing and addressing risks, researchers can ensure that the trial remains ethical, compliant, and focused on safeguarding participant well-being while generating reliable and meaningful data.

CHAPTER 5

Data Analysis and Interpretation

S tatistical methods are essential tools for analyzing and interpreting data in clinical research. They help researchers draw meaningful conclusions and make informed decisions based on the study findings. Conducting a clinical trial is a complex and resource-intensive process that involves meticulous planning, patient recruitment, data collection, and rigorous oversight. However, the true value of all this effort lies in the ability to accurately interpret the study results. Interpretation is where raw data transforms into meaningful insights that inform clinical practice, regulatory decisions, and future research. Without proper analysis and understanding, even the most well-executed trial cannot drive scientific progress or improve patient outcomes.

In this chapter, we will explore why interpreting study results is crucial, the key factors involved in the interpretation process, and how accurate interpretation impacts patient care, public health, and the broader medical community. Interpreting study results is the bridge between clinical research and real-world medical application. It is the process through which researchers extract conclusions about a treatment's safety, efficacy, and potential risks. Accurate interpretation is essential for several reasons:

Physicians and other healthcare providers rely on clinical trial outcomes to guide treatment decisions and provide the best care to patients. Misinterpreted results can lead to ineffective or harmful treatments being used in practice. Regulatory agencies, such as the U.S. Food and Drug Administration (FDA) and the European Medicines Agency (EMA), base their approval of new drugs and therapies on a clear and accurate analysis of trial outcomes. Ambiguous or misleading interpretations can delay or prevent the introduction of life-saving treatments. A thorough understanding of the data allows researchers to identify potential risks and side effects. Clear, well-interpreted results protect patients by ensuring that treatments are both safe and effective. Every clinical trial adds to the body of medical knowledge. Accurate interpretation supports future research by providing reliable evidence that can be built upon in subsequent studies. Misinterpretation of results can lead to wasted resources, as ineffective therapies may proceed to later trial phases or reach the market. Accurate interpretation ensures that investments in research yield meaningful and practical outcomes.

Interpreting study results goes beyond reporting whether a treatment "worked" or not. It requires a nuanced understanding of the trial's design, statistical analysis, and broader scientific context. The following components are critical to proper interpretation:

Statistical Significance vs. Clinical Significance

Statistical significance and clinical significance are both important concepts in clinical research, but they answer different questions. Statistical significance tells us whether the results observed in a study are likely due to an actual effect rather than random chance. This is often determined using a p-value, with a threshold of $p < 0.05$ commonly used to indicate that the findings are statistically significant. In simple terms, if a study reports a statistically significant result, it suggests that the observed difference (such as between a treatment and placebo) is unlikely to have happened by coincidence.

However, just because a result is statistically significant doesn't automatically mean it is important in real-world medical practice. This is where clinical significance comes in. Clinical significance refers to whether the difference or improvement shown in the study is large enough to make a real, meaningful difference in patients' lives. For example, a new drug might statistically reduce systolic blood pressure by 2 mmHg compared to standard treatment. While this reduction might meet the threshold for statistical significance, it may not be large enough to reduce the risk of heart attacks or strokes—outcomes that matter to patients and healthcare providers. Therefore, while the numbers show an effect, its clinical impact may be minimal or negligible.

In interpreting research results, it is important to balance these two concepts. A finding can be statistically significant but not clinically meaningful, and vice versa. For instance, in smaller studies, a large and important health benefit might not reach statistical significance simply due to insufficient sample size. Conversely, large trials can detect very small differences that are statistically significant but offer little practical benefit. Effective clinical research requires looking beyond p-values and asking: Does this intervention truly improve patient outcomes in a way that is meaningful and justifies its use in practice? Both statistical and clinical significance are needed to guide evidence-based healthcare decisions.

Understanding Effect Size

Understanding effect size is essential for interpreting the real-world impact of research findings. While statistical significance tells us whether an effect is likely to be real and not due to chance, it doesn't tell us how big that effect is—and that's where effect size comes in. Effect size quantifies the magnitude of a treatment's impact, giving clinicians, patients, and researchers a sense of how meaningful the difference is. For instance, in cancer treatment, a therapy that extends patient survival by six months is generally considered to have a larger and more clinically valuable effect size than one that only extends survival by two weeks, even if both results are statistically significant.

There are several common ways to measure effect size in clinical research, each suited for different types of outcomes. Relative Risk (RR) is often used in studies comparing the probability of an event happening in the treatment group versus the control group. For example, if the RR is 0.7, it suggests a 30% reduction in risk with treatment. Odds Ratio (OR) is similar but compares the odds, rather than the probability, of an event occurring in the treatment group compared to the control group. This measure is frequently used in case-control studies and logistic regression models. Hazard Ratio (HR), on the other hand, is used in time-to-event analyses, such as survival studies, to compare the rate at which an event (like death or disease progression) occurs in different groups over time. An HR of 0.5, for example, indicates that the event rate is halved in the treatment group compared to the control group.

Beyond these ratios, there are also absolute measures of effect size, such as risk difference (the absolute difference in event rates between groups) and number needed to treat (NNT), which tells us how many patients need to be treated to prevent one additional adverse event. Together, effect size measures provide the critical context needed to evaluate whether a treatment offers a substantial benefit that justifies its costs, side effects, or risks. Understanding both the existence (statistical significance) and magnitude (effect size) of treatment effects is key to making informed, evidence-based decisions in clinical practice.

Interpreting Confidence Intervals

Confidence intervals (CIs) provide a range of values within which the true effect likely falls. A 95% confidence interval means we can be 95% certain that the true effect lies within that range. Narrow CIs suggest greater precision, while wide CIs indicate more uncertainty.

For instance, if a drug's hazard ratio for death is 0.75 (95% CI: 0.60-0.90), the treatment reduces the risk of death by 25%, and we are fairly confident in this estimate. If the CI includes 1.0, it suggests the result may not be statistically significant.

Many trials conduct subgroup analyses to determine if certain populations respond differently to treatment (e.g., by age, sex, or ethnicity). Proper interpretation ensures that these analyses are hypothesis-generating rather than definitive. Over-reliance on subgroup results can lead to incorrect conclusions.

Generalizability (or external validity) refers to how well study results apply to populations beyond the study sample. If a trial only includes middle-aged white men, the findings may not apply to women or racially diverse groups.

Accounting for Bias and Confounding Variables

Bias and confounding variables are critical factors that can distort the outcomes of a study, leading to inaccurate conclusions. Bias refers to systematic errors that skew the results away from the true effect, while confounding variables can mask or exaggerate the relationship between the treatment and the outcome. Proper interpretation of clinical trial results requires a careful and deliberate effort to identify and address these sources of error. Some of the most common biases include selection bias, which occurs when the study population is not representative of the broader patient community, limiting the generalizability of the results. Reporting bias is another major concern—it happens when only positive or favorable results are published, while negative or inconclusive findings remain hidden from the public and the scientific community, leading to an incomplete and misleading evidence base. Attrition bias arises when participants drop out of a study at different rates between the treatment and control groups, potentially skewing the results if those who leave differ systematically from those who stay.

To interpret study results effectively, it is important to follow a structured approach. Start by carefully reviewing the study design. Was the study randomized, controlled, and double-blinded? These features are gold standards in clinical research because they help minimize bias and increase the reliability and validity of the findings. Next, examine the primary endpoint—the main question the trial aimed to answer. For example, was the trial designed to measure overall survival, disease progression, or symptom improvement? Keeping the primary endpoint in focus helps anchor your interpretation. Then, analyze the statistical methods used in the study. Check whether appropriate statistical tests were applied, whether adjustments were made for confounding factors, and whether the sample size was large enough to detect meaningful differences. But remember, numbers alone are not enough—consider the clinical relevance of the findings. A result can be statistically significant but not clinically meaningful, so always ask whether the findings will make a real difference in patient care or public health practice.

It is equally important to evaluate the limitations of the study. No study is perfect, so identifying weaknesses, such as small sample size, short follow-up period, or high dropout rates, will help you assess the strength and reliability of the conclusions. Compare the results with existing evidence. Do the findings align with previous studies, or do they contradict the established body of knowledge? Consistency with prior research lends credibility to the results, while discrepancies warrant closer examination to understand why differences exist.

The consequences of misinterpreting study results are serious and far-reaching. For patients, flawed interpretations can lead to the adoption of treatments that are unsafe or ineffective, potentially causing harm rather than benefit. At the policy level, public health initiatives may be based on faulty data, leading to programs that fail to address community needs or even cause unintended negative outcomes. Moreover, repeated misinterpretation and miscommunication of scientific results can erode public trust in clinical research and in healthcare institutions. Economically, there is a significant cost, both in wasted resources and in lost opportunities. Pharmaceutical companies, healthcare systems, and insurers may invest in interventions that do not provide true value, diverting funds from more effective solutions.

Interpreting study results is not just a technical step; it is the heart of the clinical research process. This is where raw data is transformed into actionable insights that shape patient care, inform evidence-based policies, and drive the direction of future research. To master this skill, professionals must develop a deep understanding of both statistical principles and clinical relevance and place every new finding within the broader scientific and societal context. When done well, interpretation turns data into impact, making a real difference in the lives of patients and in the health of communities.

By ensuring accurate and thoughtful interpretation of study results, clinical researchers uphold one of their most vital ethical responsibilities: to advance medical knowledge while safeguarding the welfare of patients and the broader community. Every data point collected in a study represents not just numbers, but real people who have entrusted researchers with their health and their hopes. Misinterpretation can compromise that trust and lead to misguided treatments, while careful and rigorous analysis honors the sacrifices participants make and drives real progress in medicine.

As you continue your journey in clinical research, keep in mind that the true power of your work lies not only in designing trials or generating data, but in what you do with that data. It is through thoughtful interpretation that evidence is transformed into meaningful, actionable insights that can change clinical practice, improve patient outcomes, and shape public health policy. This is where your contribution has the potential to be truly life-changing, turning research findings into real-world solutions that touch lives and make healthcare more effective, equitable, and compassionate.

So, as you take on new studies and analyze new results, approach each one with a sense of responsibility and purpose. Your role is not just to report what the data shows, but to unlock its full meaning and impact. When you interpret with care, integrity, and a commitment to truth, you fulfill the highest calling of clinical research—and help create a healthier, better-informed world.

Descriptive Statistics

Descriptive statistics summarize and describe the characteristics of the study population and key variables using measures such as mean, median, mode, and standard deviation. Descriptive statistics are fundamental tools in clinical research that provide a summary and overview of the characteristics of the study population and key variables. These statistics are essential for understanding the basic features of the data and for presenting a clear and concise description of the sample involved in the study.

One of the primary measures used in descriptive statistics is the mean, which represents the average value of a variable within the study population. By calculating the mean, researchers can get a central value around which the data points are distributed, providing a snapshot of the general trend within the sample. Alongside the mean, the median is another critical measure. The median, which is the middle value when the data is ordered from lowest to highest, is especially useful for understanding the distribution of data when it is skewed or contains outliers. It provides a better measure of central tendency in cases where extreme values might distort the mean.

The mode is another descriptive statistic that identifies the most frequently occurring value within the dataset. While it may not always be as informative as the mean or median, the mode is valuable for understanding the most common characteristics or responses in the study population.

The standard deviation is a measure of variability that indicates how spread out the values are around the mean. A high standard deviation signifies that the data points are widely dispersed from the average, while a low standard deviation indicates that the values are closely clustered around the mean. This measure is crucial for understanding the degree of variability within the study population and for assessing the reliability and consistency of the data.

By employing these descriptive statistics, researchers can effectively summarize and describe the key features of their study population, including central tendencies and variations. This initial analysis lays the groundwork for more advanced statistical techniques and helps in interpreting the results in the context of the broader research objectives.

Inferential Statistics

Inferential statistics make inferences or generalizations about a population based on sample data. Techniques include hypothesis testing, confidence intervals, and regression analysis. Inferential statistics play a pivotal role in clinical research by allowing researchers to draw conclusions and make generalizations about a larger population based on the data collected from a sample. Unlike descriptive statistics, which focus on summarizing and presenting the characteristics of the sample itself, inferential statistics enable researchers to infer properties of the broader population from which the sample is drawn.

One fundamental technique in inferential statistics is hypothesis testing, which involves making and evaluating predictions about a population based on sample data. Researchers start with a null hypothesis (typically suggesting no effect or no difference) and an alternative hypothesis (indicating the presence of an effect or difference). Through statistical tests, such as t-tests or chi-square tests, researchers determine whether the observed data provides enough evidence to reject the null hypothesis in favor of the alternative hypothesis. Hypothesis testing helps to assess the statistical significance of the results and to understand whether the observed effects are likely to be genuine or occurred by chance.

Confidence intervals are another critical component of inferential statistics. A confidence interval provides a range of values within which the true population parameter is expected to fall, with a certain level of confidence (usually 95% or 99%). For example, a 95% confidence interval for a mean would indicate that there is a 95% probability that the interval contains the true mean of the population. Confidence intervals offer valuable insight into the precision and reliability of the sample estimates and help in understanding the degree of uncertainty associated with the findings.

Regression analysis is a technique used to examine the relationships between variables and to predict outcomes based on these relationships. By fitting a regression model to the data, researchers can assess how changes in one or more independent variables (predictors) are associated with changes in a dependent variable (outcome). Regression analysis can be used for various purposes, including identifying risk factors, evaluating the impact of interventions, and making predictions about future outcomes. Techniques such as linear regression, logistic regression, and multiple regression provide insights into the nature and strength of these relationships.

Overall, inferential statistics provide the tools needed to make well-supported generalizations and predictions about a population based on sample data. These techniques are essential for testing hypotheses, estimating population parameters, and understanding the relationships between variables, thereby facilitating informed decision-making and advancing scientific knowledge in clinical research.

Survival Analysis

Survival analysis evaluates the time until a specific event occurs (e.g., death, disease progression) using methods such as Kaplan-Meier curves and Cox proportional hazards models. Survival analysis is a specialized statistical technique used to evaluate the time until a specific event of interest occurs, such as death, disease progression, or recovery. This type of analysis is particularly valuable in clinical research, where understanding the duration of time until an event happens can provide critical insights into the efficacy of treatments and the natural history of diseases.

One of the primary tools in survival analysis is the Kaplan-Meier curve, which provides a graphical representation of the survival experience of a cohort over time. The Kaplan-Meier method estimates the probability of surviving past certain time points and can accommodate censored data, which refers to instances where participants leave the study before the event occurs or are lost to follow-up. By plotting the survival probabilities against time, Kaplan-Meier curves allow researchers to visualize and compare survival rates between different groups, such as those receiving different treatments or those with different disease stages. The curves can illustrate differences in survival outcomes and provide a straightforward method for comparing the effectiveness of interventions.

Another important technique in survival analysis is the Cox proportional hazards model, which is used to assess the effect of various covariates on the hazard or risk of the event occurring. Unlike the Kaplan-Meier curve, which provides a univariate analysis, the Cox model is a multivariate approach that allows for the inclusion of multiple predictors simultaneously. This model evaluates how different factors—such as age, gender, treatment type, or baseline health status—affect the hazard rate or risk of the event. By estimating hazard ratios, the Cox model helps in understanding the relative risk of the event occurring for different levels of covariates, thereby providing a deeper insight into the factors influencing survival.

Survival analysis is crucial for understanding the time dynamics of clinical outcomes and making evidence-based decisions. By applying Kaplan-Meier curves and Cox proportional hazards models, researchers can gain valuable insights into the effectiveness of treatments, the impact of various factors on patient outcomes, and the overall prognosis of diseases. These methods help to translate time-to-event data into meaningful information that can guide clinical practice, inform patient management strategies, and contribute to the advancement of medical knowledge.

Meta-Analysis

Meta-analysis combines and analyzes data from multiple studies to derive overall conclusions and assess treatment effects across different populations. Meta-analysis is a powerful statistical technique used to combine and analyze data from multiple individual studies to derive overarching conclusions and evaluate treatment effects across diverse populations. This method enhances the robustness of research findings by aggregating results from various studies, thereby increasing the overall sample size and statistical power. Meta-analysis is particularly valuable in fields like clinical research, where individual studies may have limited sample sizes and varying methodologies that can impact the generalizability of results.

The process of conducting a meta-analysis begins with a systematic review of the literature to identify relevant studies that meet pre-specified inclusion criteria. This involves a thorough search of databases, assessment of study quality, and extraction of data from each study. Once the studies are selected, the meta-analysis combines the effect sizes reported in the individual studies to produce a pooled estimate of the treatment effect. This pooling is typically done using weighted averages, where studies with larger sample sizes or more precise estimates are given more influence in the final result.

One of the key advantages of meta-analysis is its ability to resolve discrepancies between studies and provide a more accurate estimate of the treatment effect. By analyzing data from multiple studies, researchers can account for variability and identify patterns or trends that might not be apparent in single studies. Additionally, meta-analysis can assess the consistency of results across different study populations, settings, and methodologies, thereby enhancing the generalizability of the findings.

Meta-analysis allows for the exploration of heterogeneity, or the variability in study outcomes. Researchers can investigate factors that contribute to differences in results, such as variations in study design, participant characteristics, or intervention protocols. Techniques like subgroup analysis and sensitivity analysis can be employed to examine how these factors influence the overall effect and to ensure that the conclusions drawn are robust and reliable. Meta-analysis is a crucial tool in clinical research that synthesizes data from multiple studies to provide comprehensive insights into treatment effects and research questions. By combining evidence from various sources, meta-analysis helps to establish a more definitive understanding of interventions, identify effective treatments, and guide clinical practice and policy decisions.

Statistical software plays a crucial role in modern clinical research by providing the tools necessary for data analysis, statistical modeling, and visualization. Programs such as SAS, SPSS, R, and STATA are essential for handling complex datasets and conducting sophisticated analyses that drive research conclusions and decision-making.

SAS (Statistical Analysis System) is a comprehensive software suite used for advanced analytics, multivariate analysis, and data management. It is widely employed in clinical research for its robust data manipulation capabilities and its ability to handle large datasets efficiently. SAS offers a range of procedures for statistical analysis, including regression, survival analysis, and hypothesis testing. Its extensive documentation and support make it a popular choice for both academic and industry researchers.

SPSS (Statistical Package for the Social Sciences) is known for its user-friendly interface and ease of use, making it a preferred tool for researchers who may not have extensive statistical backgrounds. SPSS provides a wide range of statistical functions, including descriptive statistics, ANOVA, and factor analysis. It is particularly useful for data entry and management, as well as for generating reports and visualizations that aid in the interpretation of results.

R is an open-source programming language and software environment that excels in statistical computing and graphics. Its flexibility and extensibility make it a powerful tool for conducting complex statistical analyses and developing custom models. R's comprehensive library of packages allows researchers to perform specialized analyses, such as meta-analysis and machine learning, and to create high-quality visualizations. The collaborative nature of R's user community also contributes to its continuous development and improvement.

STATA is another versatile statistical software package that is valued for its data analysis and manipulation capabilities. STATA offers a wide range of statistical techniques, including regression analysis, survival analysis, and panel data analysis. Its intuitive interface and robust programming features make it a valuable tool for both novice and experienced researchers. STATA's strengths lie in its ability to manage and analyze large datasets and its support for advanced statistical modeling.

Each of these statistical software packages brings unique strengths to clinical research, enabling researchers to analyze data efficiently, test hypotheses rigorously, and visualize findings effectively. By leveraging these tools, researchers can ensure that their analyses are accurate, comprehensive, and aligned with the goals of their studies. The role of statistical software is pivotal in transforming raw data into meaningful insights that drive evidence-based decisions and advance scientific knowledge.

Data Visualization

Data visualization is an essential aspect of data analysis that involves presenting data through graphs, charts, and tables to enhance the interpretation and communication of research findings. Effective visualization transforms complex datasets into intuitive, visual representations that make it easier for researchers, stakeholders, and the general public to understand and draw conclusions from the data. Graphs and charts are powerful tools for summarizing and illustrating data trends, patterns, and relationships. For example, line graphs can effectively depict changes over time, allowing researchers to observe temporal trends and fluctuations. Bar charts are useful for comparing different groups or categories, providing a clear view of relative sizes or frequencies. Pie charts offer a straightforward way to represent proportions and percentages, making it easy to see the distribution of parts within a whole. Scatter plots are employed to examine the relationship between two continuous variables, revealing correlations and potential outliers.

Tables complement graphical representations by presenting detailed numerical data in a structured format. They are particularly useful for displaying precise values and allowing for easy comparison across multiple variables or groups. Well-designed tables can effectively communicate complex information in a compact and accessible manner, facilitating detailed scrutiny and comparison. Effective data visualization also involves attention to design principles to ensure clarity and accuracy. Choosing appropriate scales, labels, and colors enhances the readability of visualizations and prevents misinterpretation. For instance, using consistent scales and clear axis labels helps avoid confusion and ensures that the visual accurately represents the underlying data. Color coding can be employed to distinguish between different groups or categories, but it should be used judiciously to avoid overwhelming the viewer or misrepresenting the data.

By leveraging data visualization, researchers can convey their findings more effectively, making complex information more accessible and comprehensible. Visualizations help in identifying trends, communicating results to non-expert audiences, and making informed decisions based on data. In clinical research, where data can be intricate and voluminous, visualization plays a critical role in summarizing results, highlighting key insights, and facilitating discussions about the implications of the research. Overall, data visualization is a crucial tool for enhancing the clarity, impact, and dissemination of research findings.

Interpreting Study Results and Drawing Conclusions

Interpreting study results involves analyzing data within the context of the study objectives and drawing valid conclusions based on statistical significance, clinical relevance, and study limitations. Interpreting study results is a critical process in clinical research that involves analyzing data in light of the study's objectives and drawing valid, evidence-based conclusions. This process requires a thorough understanding of both the statistical findings and their practical implications to ensure that the conclusions are meaningful and actionable.

The first step in interpreting results is to evaluate statistical significance. Statistical tests determine whether the observed effects or relationships are unlikely to have occurred by chance. For instance, p-values help assess whether differences between groups or associations between variables are statistically significant, typically with a threshold of 0.05. However, statistical significance alone does not imply that the results are practically important or clinically relevant. Researchers must also consider the effect size, which measures the magnitude of the observed effect. A small effect size may be statistically significant but not substantial enough to warrant clinical or practical significance.

Clinical relevance is another crucial aspect of interpreting study results. This involves assessing whether the findings have meaningful implications for patient care or clinical practice. For example, even if a treatment shows a statistically significant improvement in outcomes, it is important to evaluate whether the improvement is large enough to impact patient quality of life or change clinical guidelines. The relevance of the results should be considered in the context of the study population, treatment modalities, and the overall clinical setting.

Researchers also need to account for study limitations when drawing conclusions. Every study has inherent limitations, such as sample size, study design constraints, or potential biases. It is important to critically appraise these limitations and understand how they might affect the validity and generalizability of the findings. For instance, a study with a small sample size might have limited power to detect small effects, while a study with a high dropout rate might introduce bias that skews the results. Interpreting study results involves a comprehensive analysis of both statistical and clinical aspects to draw meaningful conclusions. Researchers must consider statistical significance, effect size, clinical relevance, and study limitations to ensure that their findings are accurate, relevant, and applicable to real-world settings. This careful interpretation helps in translating research data into actionable insights that can advance medical knowledge and improve patient outcomes.

When conducting a clinical study, it is crucial to acknowledge and discuss any limitations or biases that may have influenced the results.

Potential limitations might include the study's sample size, which could affect the generalizability of the findings, selection bias, or confounding variables that were not controlled for. Addressing these factors allows for a more accurate interpretation of the study's outcomes and provides transparency for future research considerations.

In addition to identifying study limitations, it is essential to contextualize the findings within the broader landscape of existing literature and clinical practice guidelines. This approach helps to understand the study's implications for patient care and highlights areas where further research may be needed. By comparing the study's results with existing data, researchers can assess the consistency of their findings and explore how they contribute to the evolving body of knowledge.

Real-World Evidence (RWE) and Comparative Effectiveness Research (CER) play a significant role in complementing traditional clinical trials. RWE provides valuable insights into how interventions are performed in real-world settings, while CER compares the effectiveness of different treatment options. RWE is derived from various sources, including electronic health records (EHRs), claims databases, and patient registries, offering a more comprehensive view of treatment outcomes across diverse patient populations. This evidence is vital for informing regulatory decisions, healthcare policy, and clinical practice guidelines, particularly regarding the long-term safety, effectiveness, and cost-effectiveness of interventions.

On the other hand, Comparative Effectiveness Research (CER) focuses on comparing the effectiveness of different interventions, such as drugs or procedures, in real-world settings. The objective is to provide healthcare decision-makers with evidence that can guide treatment choices. CER employs methods like observational studies, pragmatic trials, and systematic reviews to evaluate outcomes, including mortality, morbidity, quality of life, and healthcare utilization.

Regulatory submissions are critical milestones in the drug development process, requiring a thorough analysis and interpretation of data to support claims of safety and efficacy. These submissions often include a New Drug Application (NDA) or Biologics License Application (BLA), which compiles data from preclinical and clinical studies, including study protocols, results, safety data, and manufacturing information. Clinical Study Reports (CSRs) are also integral components of regulatory submissions, summarizing the design, conduct, results, and conclusions of clinical trials in a structured format for regulatory review. Additionally, Statistical Analysis Plans (SAPs) detail the statistical methods used to analyze study data, ensuring transparency and reproducibility of the results.

The approval process involves a rigorous review by regulatory authorities, such as the FDA or EMA, to assess the safety, efficacy, and quality of the investigational product. In some cases, advisory committees comprising experts in the field are consulted to evaluate specific aspects of the data or study design. Post-approval commitments, such as additional studies or surveillance activities, are often required to continue monitoring the product's safety and effectiveness in the broader population.

CHAPTER 6

Career Development in Clinical Research

Navigating your career path in clinical research requires strategic planning and a commitment to continuous learning. To build a successful career in this field, it's essential to understand the wide range of career options available, pursue relevant certifications and professional development opportunities, actively engage in networking and seek out mentorship, and develop strong negotiation skills for salaries and career advancement.

Clinical research offers a diverse array of career opportunities, each playing a vital role in the successful conduct of clinical trials and the broader advancement of healthcare. Key roles include Clinical Research Associates (CRAs), who monitor the progress of clinical trials to ensure compliance with protocols and regulatory requirements; Project Managers, who oversee the planning, execution, and completion of clinical research projects, ensuring they stay on schedule and within budget; and Regulatory Affairs Specialists, who focus on the regulatory aspects of clinical trials, ensuring that studies meet all legal and ethical standards. These roles, among others, provide multiple avenues for professionals to contribute meaningfully to the field, depending on their skills, interests, and career goals.

To advance in clinical research, obtaining relevant certifications and engaging in continuous professional development is crucial. Some clinical research certifications can enhance your credentials and demonstrate your expertise to potential employers. Additionally, staying up-to-date with the latest developments in clinical research through workshops, webinars, and conferences will keep your skills sharp and make you more competitive in the job market. Continuous learning is key to staying ahead in a field that is constantly evolving with new technologies, regulations, and methodologies.

Building a robust professional network and seeking out mentorship are critical components of career development in clinical research. Networking can open doors to job opportunities, collaborations, and partnerships that may not be advertised publicly. Attending industry conferences, joining professional organizations, and participating in online forums are effective ways to connect with peers and industry leaders. Mentorship, on the other hand, provides guidance and insight from those who have navigated the field successfully. A mentor can offer advice on career decisions, help you navigate challenges, and provide valuable industry knowledge, making your career progression smoother and more informed.

Effective negotiation skills are essential when it comes to securing a competitive salary and advancing in your career. Understanding the market rates for various roles in clinical research and being able to articulate your value based on your skills, experience, and certifications are key to successful salary negotiations. Additionally, career advancement often requires strategic moves, such as pursuing roles that offer greater responsibility, seeking out leadership opportunities, and continuously upgrading your skills. Being proactive about your career progression and willing to take calculated risks can lead to significant long-term rewards in the form of higher positions and better compensation.

By strategically navigating these aspects of your career path, you can build a successful and fulfilling career in clinical research, making meaningful contributions to the field while achieving your personal and professional goals. Navigating a career in clinical research requires proactive career planning, continuous learning, and leveraging networking and mentorship opportunities. By investing in certifications, professional development, and strategic career advancement strategies, you can build a rewarding and successful career in this dynamic field.

CHAPTER 7

Challenges and Future Trends in Clinical Research

Importance of Diversity

Diversity in clinical research is vital to ensuring that medical treatments and interventions are effective and safe for all populations. Representation is a cornerstone of this effort, as it requires the inclusion of diverse populations based on key demographic factors such as age, race, ethnicity, socioeconomic status, and geographic location. When clinical trials include participants from varied backgrounds, the data collected is more likely to reflect the real-world population, leading to findings that are more generalizable and applicable across different groups.

This inclusive approach helps to address health disparities and ensures that no group is left behind in the advancement of medical science. For instance, certain medical conditions and treatment responses can vary significantly across different demographic groups due to genetic, environmental, and social factors. By incorporating a wide range of participants, researchers can identify these differences early on, leading to more personalized and effective healthcare solutions. Furthermore, the inclusion of diverse populations in clinical trials helps build trust within communities that have historically been underrepresented or marginalized in research. It signals a commitment to equity and fairness in the pursuit of better health outcomes for all. In sum, the importance of diversity in clinical research cannot be overstated; it is essential for developing treatments that are safe, effective, and accessible to everyone, regardless of their background.

Health Disparities

Addressing health disparities in clinical research is crucial to ensuring that investigational therapies are effective across diverse patient groups. Health disparities—differences in health outcomes and access to care that are often linked to social, economic, and environmental factors—can lead to certain populations being disproportionately affected by diseases and less likely to benefit from medical advancements. By intentionally focusing on these disparities within clinical trials, researchers can work to develop therapies that are not only effective but also equitable.

Ensuring that investigational therapies work across diverse patient groups involves including a wide range of participants in clinical trials, particularly those from historically underserved and marginalized communities. This approach helps to identify variations in how different groups respond to treatments, which may be influenced by factors such as genetics, lifestyle, and access to healthcare. Without this diversity in trial participants, therapies may be approved based on data that does not fully represent the broader population, potentially leading to less effective or even harmful outcomes for certain groups.

Addressing health disparities in clinical research goes beyond just improving individual patient outcomes; it also plays a role in reducing overall healthcare inequities. When therapies are developed and tested with a focus on inclusivity, the resulting treatments are more likely to benefit all populations, contributing to a fairer distribution of healthcare resources. This approach is not only a matter of scientific accuracy but also of social justice, ensuring that everyone has the opportunity to receive the best possible care, regardless of their background. By prioritizing the inclusion of diverse patient groups in clinical research, the medical community can work toward eliminating health disparities and achieving more equitable health outcomes for all.

Community Engagement

Community engagement is a vital component of increasing awareness and participation in clinical trials. By partnering with community organizations, researchers can build trust and foster relationships with diverse populations, who may otherwise be hesitant or unaware of the opportunities to participate in clinical research. These partnerships allow for a more effective dissemination of information about the purpose, benefits, and safety of clinical trials, tailored to the specific needs and concerns of the community.

Engaging with community organizations also provides a platform for addressing potential barriers to participation, such as mistrust in the medical system, lack of access to healthcare, and cultural differences. By working collaboratively with trusted community leaders and organizations, researchers can better understand these barriers and develop strategies to overcome them. This could include hosting informational sessions, offering translation services, or addressing transportation issues to make trial participation more accessible.

Community engagement helps ensure that the voices and perspectives of underrepresented groups are included in the research process. This inclusion can lead to more relevant and impactful research outcomes, as the trials will more accurately reflect the needs and experiences of the broader population. Ultimately, by partnering with community organizations, researchers can enhance the diversity of clinical trial participants, improve the generalizability of study results, and contribute to reducing health disparities.

Cultural Competence

Cultural competence is essential in conducting effective and inclusive clinical trials. It involves training study staff to understand and respect the cultural nuances of the diverse populations they engage with. This understanding is critical, as it allows researchers and study teams to build trust, communicate more effectively, and address the unique needs and concerns of participants from various cultural backgrounds.

Training in cultural competence equips study staff with the skills to navigate cultural differences, including language barriers, varying health beliefs, and different levels of comfort with medical research. By being culturally sensitive, study teams can tailor their communication strategies and interactions to resonate with participants, ensuring that they feel respected and understood throughout the research process. This approach not only enhances participant engagement but also helps to mitigate potential misunderstandings or mistrust that could hinder participation.

Cultural competence is crucial for ensuring that the study design and implementation are inclusive and respectful of the diverse populations involved. It enables researchers to consider cultural factors that may influence health behaviors, treatment outcomes, and participant experiences, leading to more accurate and meaningful research findings. Ultimately, by fostering cultural competence within study teams, clinical trials can be more inclusive, ethical, and effective, contributing to better health outcomes for all communities involved.

Incorporating Digital Health Technologies and Artificial Intelligence

Incorporating digital health technologies and artificial intelligence (AI) into clinical trials presents a transformative opportunity to streamline the research process and significantly enhance data collection and analysis. Digital health technologies, such as wearable devices, mobile health apps, and remote monitoring tools, enable real-time data collection from participants, providing a more comprehensive and continuous picture of their health status. These technologies facilitate more efficient patient monitoring, improve adherence to study protocols, and allow for the collection of vast amounts of data that were previously difficult or impossible to obtain in traditional clinical trials.

Artificial intelligence further amplifies the potential of these technologies by enabling the rapid analysis of large and complex datasets. AI algorithms can identify patterns, predict outcomes, and uncover insights that might be missed through manual analysis. This capability not only accelerates the pace of research but also enhances the precision and accuracy of findings. For instance, AI can be used to optimize patient recruitment by identifying eligible participants more efficiently, reducing the time and cost associated with this critical phase of clinical trials. Additionally, AI-driven analytics can assist in the early detection of adverse events, ensuring that potential risks are identified and addressed promptly.

By integrating digital health technologies and AI, clinical trials can become more adaptive, patient-centered, and data-rich. This integration ultimately leads to more robust and generalizable results, faster trial completion times, and the potential for personalized treatment approaches that are informed by real-time data. As the landscape of clinical research continues to evolve, embracing these technological advancements will be key to improving the efficiency, effectiveness, and inclusivity of clinical trials, ultimately contributing to better health outcomes for diverse patient populations.

Digital Health Technologies

Digital health technologies, particularly remote monitoring tools, are revolutionizing the way clinical trials are conducted by enhancing participant compliance and data accuracy. Wearable devices, such as fitness trackers and smartwatches, along with mobile health apps, enable the continuous collection of patient data outside of traditional clinical settings. This real-time monitoring allows researchers to gather comprehensive information on patients' health metrics, such as heart rate, physical activity, sleep patterns, and other vital signs, throughout the trial period.

The ability to monitor patients remotely not only reduces the need for frequent in-person visits but also increases the accuracy and reliability of the data collected. Participants are more likely to adhere to study protocols when their daily routines are minimally disrupted, and the data captured is less prone to recall bias or errors associated with self-reporting. Additionally, remote monitoring facilitates the early detection of any deviations from expected outcomes, enabling timely interventions and improving overall patient safety. By leveraging these digital health technologies, clinical trials can achieve higher levels of efficiency, data integrity, and patient engagement, ultimately leading to more meaningful and actionable research outcomes.

Integrate Electronic Health Record EHR data to streamline patient recruitment, identify eligible participants, and collect real-world evidence. Leverage the integration of (EHR) data to streamline patient recruitment by efficiently identifying eligible participants based on pre-defined clinical criteria, improving enrollment timelines, and enhancing trial diversity. Additionally, utilize EHR systems to collect real-world evidence (RWE) throughout the study, enabling more accurate insights into patient outcomes, treatment effectiveness, and long-term safety in real-world clinical settings.

Artificial Intelligence

Artificial Intelligence (AI) is transforming the landscape of clinical trials by introducing predictive analytics, a powerful tool that enhances the efficiency and effectiveness of research. Through AI algorithms, researchers can predict patient outcomes with remarkable accuracy, helping to identify which patients are most likely to benefit from a particular treatment. This capability allows for more personalized and targeted approaches to clinical trial design, ensuring that the right patients are enrolled and that the study is set up for success from the start.

AI-driven predictive analytics can optimize trial design by analyzing vast amounts of data from previous studies, patient records, and real-world evidence. These insights enable researchers to anticipate potential challenges, such as patient dropout or unexpected adverse events, and adjust protocols accordingly. By forecasting risks and identifying adverse events before they occur, AI can significantly enhance patient safety and reduce the likelihood of costly trial delays. Ultimately, the integration of AI in clinical trials not only accelerates the research process but also improves the quality and reliability of the outcomes, paving the way for more effective and safer therapeutic interventions.

Natural Language Processing

Natural Language Processing (NLP) is a rapidly advancing field within artificial intelligence that holds significant potential for transforming clinical research, particularly in the analysis of unstructured data. Unstructured data, which includes information found in medical records, patient reports, clinical notes, and even social media posts, represents a vast and often untapped resource in healthcare. Traditional data analysis methods struggle to process this type of information due to its variability and complexity. However, NLP can effectively interpret and analyze these data sources, converting them into structured, actionable insights that can enhance decision-making throughout the clinical trial process.

One of the primary applications of NLP in clinical research is the extraction of key information from electronic health records (EHRs). EHRs contain a wealth of unstructured data, such as physician notes, patient histories, and diagnostic reports, which are critical for understanding patient conditions and outcomes. NLP algorithms can sift through this information, identifying relevant patterns and correlations that might otherwise go unnoticed. For example, NLP can be used to detect early signs of disease progression, monitor patient symptoms over time, or identify potential side effects of treatments. By transforming these textual data into structured formats, researchers can integrate them with other data types, such as genetic information or imaging data, to build more comprehensive models of patient health.

NLP facilitates patient recruitment and trial matching by analyzing patient reports and medical records to identify candidates who meet specific eligibility criteria. Traditionally, this process has been manual and time-consuming, often requiring clinical staff to review individual records. NLP can automate this task, quickly scanning large volumes of data to find suitable participants, thereby speeding up the recruitment process and ensuring that trials are populated with the right patient demographics.

In addition to enhancing patient recruitment, NLP can improve the quality of data collected during clinical trials. Patient-reported outcomes (PROs), which are often recorded in free-text form, provide valuable insights into how patients perceive their treatment and its impact on their quality of life. NLP tools can analyze these reports to quantify patient sentiments, track changes over time, and correlate them with clinical outcomes. This enables researchers to gain a deeper understanding of the patient experience and to adjust treatment protocols in real-time to better meet patient needs.

NLP can assist in adverse event detection by analyzing clinical notes and patient feedback for mentions of side effects or complications. Early detection of such events is crucial for patient safety and for making timely decisions about the continuation or modification of a trial. By using NLP to monitor unstructured data streams continuously, researchers can identify emerging safety concerns more quickly than with traditional methods.

NLP also plays a significant role in literature reviews and meta-analyses, where it can be used to parse vast amounts of scientific publications, extracting relevant data points, summarizing findings, and identifying trends across studies. This capability is particularly valuable in rapidly evolving fields where staying updated with the latest research is essential for informed decision-making. NLP can automate the tedious aspects of this process, allowing researchers to focus on interpreting the results and drawing meaningful conclusions.

Finally, NLP's ability to process unstructured data extends beyond traditional text sources. It can analyze spoken language, such as patient interviews or clinician-patient interactions, to capture subtleties in tone, emotion, and context that might be missed in written reports. This adds another layer of depth to the data, providing richer insights into patient experiences and clinician practices.

In summary, Natural Language Processing (NLP) is revolutionizing the way unstructured data is utilized in clinical research. By transforming complex, free-text information into structured, actionable insights, NLP enhances decision-making across multiple stages of clinical trials, from patient recruitment and data collection to adverse event detection and literature review. As NLP technology continues to evolve, its integration into clinical research promises to unlock new levels of understanding and innovation in healthcare, ultimately leading to more effective treatments and improved patient outcomes.

Regulatory Changes and Their Impact on Research Practices

Regulatory changes in clinical research are a dynamic and critical aspect that significantly influences research practices and the overall landscape of drug development and medical innovation. As governments and regulatory bodies, such as the U.S. Food and Drug Administration (FDA) and the European Medicines Agency (EMA), continuously update and refine regulations to address emerging challenges, technological advancements, and public health needs, researchers must stay informed and adapt their practices accordingly. Navigating these regulatory changes is crucial not only for maintaining compliance but also for ensuring that clinical trials are conducted ethically, safely, and efficiently.

One of the primary impacts of regulatory changes on research practices is the need for constant vigilance and adaptability in protocol design and execution. For example, the introduction of new guidelines on patient safety, data integrity, or informed consent procedures can necessitate significant modifications to existing protocols. These changes might require additional training for research staff, revisions to study documentation, or even the re-evaluation of study endpoints. Failure to comply with updated regulations can lead to delays in trial progression, increased costs, and, in some cases, the invalidation of study results, which can have severe consequences for both the sponsor and the patients involved.

Regulatory changes often reflect broader shifts in societal expectations and ethical standards, particularly concerning patient rights and data protection. The implementation of the General Data Protection Regulation (GDPR) in the European Union, for example, introduced stringent requirements for the handling of personal data, including sensitive health information. This regulatory shift has had a profound impact on how clinical trials are conducted, requiring researchers to implement robust data protection measures, obtain explicit consent from participants, and ensure that data is processed in a manner that respects individuals' privacy rights. Such changes necessitate a thorough understanding of legal requirements and often involve collaboration with legal experts to ensure that all aspects of the trial are compliant.

In addition to ethical considerations, regulatory changes can also impact the methodologies used in clinical research. For instance, the increasing emphasis on real-world evidence (RWE) and patient-centered outcomes has led to the adoption of new regulatory frameworks that accommodate the use of data collected outside traditional clinical trial settings. This shift has encouraged researchers to explore innovative study designs, such as pragmatic trials and adaptive designs, which can better reflect real-world patient populations and treatment environments. Adapting to these methodological changes requires a deep understanding of both regulatory expectations and the scientific principles underpinning these novel approaches.

Furthermore, the global nature of clinical research adds another layer of complexity to navigating regulatory changes. Research practices must often be aligned with the requirements of multiple regulatory authorities, each with its own set of guidelines and expectations. This can create challenges in terms of harmonizing protocols, managing multi-site trials, and ensuring that all regulatory submissions meet the necessary standards. The International Council for Harmonization of Technical Requirements for Pharmaceuticals for Human Use (ICH) plays a crucial role in promoting regulatory convergence, but researchers still need to be adept at navigating the nuances of different regulatory environments.

Another significant impact of regulatory changes is on the timelines and costs associated with clinical research. New regulations often introduce additional requirements, such as increased monitoring, more rigorous documentation, or enhanced safety reporting, which can extend the duration of trials and increase operational costs. Researchers must therefore be proactive in anticipating these changes and incorporating them into their planning and budgeting processes. Effective project management and risk assessment are essential to mitigate the potential disruptions caused by regulatory shifts.

Staying abreast of regulatory changes is not just about compliance; it also presents opportunities for innovation and improvement in research practices. For example, regulatory encouragement for the use of digital health technologies and artificial intelligence (AI) in clinical trials has opened new avenues for enhancing trial efficiency, data quality, and patient engagement. Researchers who are quick to adapt to these regulatory trends can gain a competitive edge, driving advancements in drug development and ultimately delivering new therapies to patients more quickly and effectively.

Navigating regulatory changes is a critical component of clinical research that requires constant attention, adaptability, and strategic planning. These changes impact every aspect of research practices, from protocol design and data management to ethical considerations and trial methodologies. By staying informed and responsive to evolving regulatory standards, researchers can ensure that their studies are conducted in compliance with the latest guidelines, thereby safeguarding patient safety, maintaining data integrity, and contributing to the advancement of medical science.

Emerging Regulations

In the rapidly evolving landscape of clinical research, emerging regulations around data privacy are increasingly becoming a focal point, particularly with the introduction and enforcement of comprehensive frameworks such as the General Data Protection Regulation (GDPR) in the European Union. The GDPR, which came into effect in May 2018, represents a significant shift in how personal data, including sensitive health information, must be handled, stored, and processed within clinical trials and other research activities. Compliance with these regulations is not merely a legal requirement but a fundamental aspect of maintaining trust with study participants, ensuring the ethical conduct of research, and upholding the integrity of the data collected.

The GDPR sets stringent standards for data protection, requiring that any organization involved in processing personal data must do so transparently and lawfully, with the explicit consent of the individuals whose data is being used. For clinical researchers, this means that informed consent processes must be more comprehensive, ensuring that participants fully understand how their data will be used, who will have access to it, and what measures will be in place to protect their privacy.

This necessitates clear communication and documentation, with researchers needing to ensure that consent is not only obtained but also documented in a manner that is compliant with GDPR standards.

One of the key challenges presented by the GDPR and similar data privacy laws is the requirement for organizations to implement robust data protection measures. This includes the use of encryption, pseudonymization, and other technological safeguards to ensure that personal data cannot be easily traced back to individual participants. Additionally, organizations must have in place protocols for responding to data breaches, including notifying affected individuals and regulatory authorities within a specified timeframe. This aspect of compliance demands that research institutions and sponsors invest in secure data management systems and regularly review and update their data protection practices to keep pace with emerging threats and regulatory expectations.

GDPR introduces the concept of data minimization, which mandates that only the data necessary for the research purpose should be collected and processed. This has profound implications for clinical research design, as it requires researchers to critically evaluate the data they plan to collect and ensure that it is directly relevant to their study objectives. Collecting excessive or unnecessary data not only increases the risk of non-compliance but also raises ethical concerns, as it may expose participants to unnecessary risks related to data privacy. Researchers must therefore be diligent in designing studies that align with the principles of data minimization, while still achieving their scientific objectives.

Another critical aspect of GDPR compliance in clinical research is the requirement for data transparency and accountability. Organizations must maintain detailed records of data processing activities, including the legal basis for processing, the categories of data processed, and the entities with whom data is shared. This level of transparency is intended to give individuals greater control over their personal data and to ensure that organizations are accountable for their data protection practices. For clinical researchers, this means maintaining meticulous records and being prepared to demonstrate compliance in the event of an audit or investigation by regulatory authorities.

The global nature of clinical research adds an additional layer of complexity to GDPR compliance, as researchers often work across multiple jurisdictions with varying data privacy laws. While the GDPR is one of the most comprehensive data privacy regulations, other regions, including the United States, have their own sets of rules and guidelines, such as the Health Insurance Portability and Accountability Act (HIPAA). Researchers conducting multinational studies must therefore navigate a complex regulatory environment, ensuring that their practices are compliant with all relevant laws and that data transfers between countries meet the necessary legal standards. This often involves the use of contractual agreements, such as Standard Contractual Clauses (SCCs), to facilitate cross-border data transfers in a manner that complies with GDPR requirements.

The GDPR also introduces specific rights for data subjects, including the right to access their data, the right to rectify inaccuracies, and the right to have their data erased under certain circumstances (known as the "right to be forgotten"). These rights have significant implications for clinical research, particularly in terms of how data is managed throughout the study lifecycle. Researchers must have processes in place to respond to data subject requests in a timely and efficient manner, while also balancing these rights against the need to maintain data integrity for scientific purposes. For example, while a participant may request the deletion of their data, researchers must consider how this will impact the validity of the study results and whether exemptions under the GDPR allow for the retention of certain data for research purposes.

GDPR emphasizes the importance of conducting Data Protection Impact Assessments (DPIAs) for any data processing activities that are likely to result in a high risk to the rights and freedoms of individuals. In the context of clinical research, this means that before starting a study, researchers must assess the potential risks to data privacy and take steps to mitigate these risks. DPIAs are not only a regulatory requirement but also a valuable tool for identifying and addressing privacy concerns early in the research process, thereby enhancing the overall quality and ethical standards of the study.

Emerging regulations like the GDPR have a profound impact on clinical research practices, necessitating a comprehensive approach to data privacy and protection. Compliance with these regulations is essential for maintaining the trust of study participants, safeguarding sensitive health information, and ensuring the ethical conduct of research. As data privacy laws continue to evolve and expand globally, researchers must remain vigilant, continuously updating their practices and investing in the necessary tools and training to navigate this complex regulatory landscape. By doing so, they can not only meet legal requirements but also contribute to the advancement of research in a manner that respects and protects the rights of individuals.

Real-World Evidence

Real-World Evidence (RWE) is increasingly recognized as a pivotal element in supporting regulatory submissions and enhancing post-market surveillance. Unlike data derived from controlled clinical trials, RWE is generated from everyday clinical practice and reflects the outcomes and experiences of diverse patient populations in real-world settings. The acceptance of RWE by regulatory authorities such as the FDA and EMA marks a significant shift in how evidence is used to evaluate the safety and efficacy of medical interventions.

RWE encompasses data from a variety of sources, including electronic health records (EHRs), claims and billing databases, patient registries, and mobile health applications. This breadth of data provides a comprehensive view of how treatments perform outside the constraints of clinical trials, where conditions are often highly controlled and populations are more homogenous. By integrating RWE into the regulatory framework, agencies can better understand the long-term effects of interventions, assess their impact on broader patient populations, and identify any previously unrecognized risks or benefits.

The utilization of RWE is particularly valuable in post-market surveillance, where it helps in monitoring the real-world performance of medical products after their initial approval. Post-market studies and ongoing data collection through RWE can uncover insights into the effectiveness of a product across different subpopulations, address any emerging safety concerns, and inform decisions regarding label changes or additional indications. This approach ensures that medical products continue to meet the needs of patients and adapt to new challenges as they arise in everyday clinical settings.

Furthermore, the integration of RWE into regulatory submissions supports a more dynamic and responsive regulatory process. It allows for a more nuanced evaluation of how treatments perform in varied real-world scenarios, potentially accelerating the availability of new therapies and improving patient outcomes. As the landscape of healthcare evolves, the ongoing incorporation of RWE into regulatory practices is likely to enhance the ability to make informed, evidence-based decisions that better reflect the realities of patient care.

Adaptive Trial Designs

The advent of adaptive trial designs represents a transformative shift in clinical research practices, driven by increased regulatory flexibility and a focus on optimizing the efficiency and effectiveness of trials. Adaptive trial designs allow researchers to modify various aspects of a study based on interim data analysis, which can lead to more informed decision-making and potentially faster and more reliable outcomes. This approach contrasts with traditional fixed designs, where the study protocol remains static from start to finish, regardless of emerging evidence or unexpected results.

One of the primary advantages of adaptive trial designs is their ability to incorporate interim findings to refine or adjust the study parameters. This flexibility can manifest in several ways, such as altering sample sizes, changing dosing regimens, or modifying eligibility criteria in response to preliminary data. For instance, if early results indicate that a particular dosage of a drug is more effective or has fewer side effects than initially anticipated, the trial design can be adjusted to focus on this optimized dosage. Similarly, if a treatment proves ineffective, adaptive designs allow for the discontinuation of ineffective arms of the study, thus conserving resources and directing efforts toward more promising avenues.

Regulatory authorities, including the FDA and EMA, have increasingly endorsed adaptive trial designs due to their potential to enhance the scientific and ethical value of clinical research. This endorsement reflects a broader recognition that adaptive designs can accelerate the development of new therapies and improve patient outcomes by enabling more flexible and responsive research strategies. By allowing for real-time adjustments based on accumulating data, adaptive designs not only streamline the research process but also help to ensure that trials are more likely to yield meaningful and actionable results.

Adaptive trial designs contribute to better resource utilization and cost-effectiveness in clinical research. By identifying promising treatments or eliminating ineffective ones earlier in the process, adaptive designs can reduce the time and financial investments required to reach conclusive results. This efficiency is particularly valuable in high-stakes research environments where rapid advancements are critical, such as in the development of treatments for emerging health crises or rare diseases.

In practice, implementing adaptive trial designs involves careful planning and a robust statistical framework to ensure that modifications are made in a scientifically valid and ethical manner. Regulatory agencies typically require detailed proposals and justifications for planned adaptations, including how they will be implemented and how they might affect the overall validity of the trial. This rigorous oversight helps to balance the benefits of flexibility with the need to maintain the integrity and reliability of clinical research findings.

Overall, the incorporation of adaptive trial designs into research practices represents a significant advancement in clinical trial methodology. By embracing this flexible and responsive approach, researchers can better navigate the complexities of drug development, improve the likelihood of successful outcomes, and ultimately bring more effective and safer treatments to market more efficiently.

Expanded Access Programs

Expanded Access Programs (EAPs), also known as compassionate use programs, are crucial mechanisms that enable patients with serious or life-threatening conditions to gain access to investigational therapies outside the confines of formal clinical trials. These programs are designed to bridge the gap between the clinical research stage and broader public availability of new treatments, offering hope to patients who might otherwise have no viable therapeutic options.

The primary goal of Expanded Access Programs is to provide access to promising investigational drugs, biologics, or medical devices to individuals who are not eligible for ongoing clinical trials or for whom clinical trial participation is not a feasible option. These patients often suffer from severe health conditions where standard treatments have failed or are insufficient, and where the investigational therapy represents a potentially life-saving or life-improving alternative. By facilitating access to such therapies, EAPs play a critical role in addressing urgent medical needs and offering patients a chance to benefit from cutting-edge treatments that are still under development.

The process of initiating an EAP involves several steps, starting with a request from the patient or their healthcare provider to the drug manufacturer or sponsor. The manufacturer must then submit an application to regulatory authorities, such as the U.S. Food and Drug Administration (FDA) or the European Medicines Agency (EMA), detailing the safety and efficacy data of the investigational therapy and providing justification for its use outside of a clinical trial setting. This application must also include information about the potential risks, benefits, and the criteria for patient selection. Regulatory agencies review these applications to ensure that the use of the investigational therapy is justifiable and that appropriate safeguards are in place to protect patient safety.

For patients, the opportunity to participate in an EAP can be a beacon of hope in the face of serious illness. While EAPs do not guarantee that the investigational therapy will be effective or free of adverse effects, they provide a pathway to access potentially beneficial treatments that may otherwise be unavailable. Patients who receive therapy through an EAP often contribute valuable data and feedback that can further inform the development and evaluation of the investigational product.

The implementation of Expanded Access Programs also involves addressing several practical and ethical considerations. Manufacturers must ensure that they have the capacity to produce sufficient quantities of the investigational therapy to meet the demand generated by EAP requests, while maintaining quality and regulatory compliance. Additionally, healthcare providers must be well-informed about the investigational nature of the therapy, including its potential risks and benefits, and must work closely with patients to monitor their response and manage any adverse effects.

Ethically, EAPs raise important questions about fairness and equity. There is a need to balance the urgent needs of individual patients with the broader implications for clinical research and public health. Regulatory agencies and manufacturers must navigate these ethical dilemmas to ensure that expanded access is provided in a manner that is both compassionate and responsible, without compromising the integrity of the clinical development process.

Overall, Expanded Access Programs are a vital component of the drug development landscape, offering a critical avenue for patients to access investigational therapies in situations where traditional clinical trial participation is not possible. By facilitating access to promising treatments and addressing urgent medical needs, EAPs contribute significantly to advancing patient care and improving outcomes for individuals facing severe or life-threatening health conditions.

Globalization of Clinical Trials and International Collaboration

The globalization of clinical trials represents a transformative shift in the landscape of medical research, driven by the need to enhance the generalizability and applicability of findings across diverse populations and geographies. Conducting clinical trials on an international scale opens up vast opportunities for access to a broader and more varied pool of patients, enabling researchers to study interventions across different ethnicities, age groups, and socio-economic backgrounds. This diversity is crucial for understanding how therapies perform across various demographic groups, thereby improving the accuracy and relevance of clinical findings. Furthermore, international trials facilitate the integration of global expertise and resources, allowing for the pooling of knowledge, technological advancements, and specialized skills that might not be available in a single country. This collaborative approach enhances the quality of research and accelerates the development of new treatments by leveraging the strengths of multiple research hubs worldwide.

However, the globalization of clinical trials is not without its challenges. One of the primary hurdles is navigating the complex regulatory environments of different countries. Each nation has its own set of regulations governing clinical research, including ethical standards, data protection laws, and approval processes. Coordinating these diverse regulatory requirements can be cumbersome and time-consuming, potentially leading to delays in trial initiation and execution. Additionally, researchers must ensure that they comply with local laws regarding informed consent, patient privacy, and the use of medical data, which can vary significantly from one jurisdiction to another. This regulatory complexity necessitates meticulous planning and robust legal and administrative frameworks to ensure compliance across all participating countries.

Logistically, managing clinical trials across multiple countries involves addressing various operational challenges. These include coordinating the supply chain for investigational products, ensuring consistent quality control, and managing cross-border communication among study teams. Differences in healthcare infrastructure and practices can also impact the implementation and monitoring of trials, requiring adaptations to account for local variations in medical practices and patient care. Moreover, cultural differences can influence patient recruitment, engagement, and adherence to trial protocols, making it essential for researchers to develop culturally sensitive approaches and materials.

Despite these challenges, international collaboration in clinical trials offers significant advantages. It allows for faster recruitment of participants, particularly for rare diseases or conditions with low prevalence in specific regions. Global trials also facilitate the exploration of how genetic, environmental, and lifestyle factors affect the efficacy and safety of interventions, providing a more comprehensive understanding of treatment outcomes. The exchange of knowledge and best practices between international research teams fosters innovation and enhances the overall quality of clinical research.

The successful execution of global clinical trials relies on strong partnerships and effective communication between stakeholders, including pharmaceutical companies, research institutions, regulatory agencies, and healthcare providers. Building and maintaining these partnerships require careful negotiation, mutual trust, and a shared commitment to advancing medical science while respecting local customs and regulations. By addressing the logistical, regulatory, and cultural challenges associated with international collaboration, researchers can harness the full potential of global clinical trials to improve patient outcomes and advance healthcare on a worldwide scale.

Benefits of Global Trials

The expansion of clinical trials on a global scale offers profound benefits, particularly in terms of increasing access to investigational therapies for underserved populations and regions. One of the most significant advantages of global trials is their ability to bridge gaps in healthcare access, reaching patients who might otherwise be excluded from the benefits of emerging treatments. By conducting trials in diverse geographical locations, researchers can extend opportunities for participation to individuals who face barriers due to geographic isolation, limited healthcare infrastructure, or socio-economic challenges. This inclusive approach not only democratizes access to cutting-edge therapies but also ensures that new treatments are evaluated in a broader, more representative patient population, enhancing their relevance and applicability.

Access to investigational therapies in underserved regions is particularly critical for addressing health disparities and improving outcomes in areas with high unmet medical needs. Many developing countries and low-resource settings face significant challenges in accessing advanced medical treatments due to financial constraints, inadequate healthcare systems, and limited availability of innovative therapies. By incorporating these regions into global trials, researchers can offer patients in these areas the opportunity to participate in studies that might otherwise be unavailable to them. This not only provides access to potentially life-saving treatments but also contributes to the global effort to address health inequities by including diverse populations in clinical research.

Global trials help to accelerate the development and availability of new therapies by increasing the speed and scale of patient recruitment. In regions with higher patient densities or where specific conditions are more prevalent, researchers can recruit participants more quickly, which can shorten the duration of trials and expedite the delivery of new treatments to market. This is especially important for rare diseases or conditions with a low incidence in any single country, where pooling resources and participants from multiple countries can significantly enhance the efficiency of the research process.

The inclusion of a wide range of patients in global trials also allows for a more comprehensive evaluation of the safety and efficacy of investigational therapies across different populations. Variations in genetics, environmental factors, and lifestyle can influence how patients respond to treatments, and global trials provide the opportunity to assess these effects in a diverse cohort. This thorough evaluation helps to identify any potential differences in treatment response or adverse effects, leading to more tailored and effective healthcare solutions that are applicable to a global audience.

Global trials can foster collaboration between international research institutions, healthcare providers, and pharmaceutical companies, creating a network of expertise and resources that enhances the overall quality of research. These collaborations facilitate the sharing of knowledge, best practices, and technological innovations, contributing to the advancement of medical science and the improvement of patient care worldwide.

These global trials significantly enhance patient access to investigational therapies, particularly for underserved and underrepresented populations. By including diverse geographic regions and patient groups in clinical research, these trials address health disparities, accelerate the development of new treatments, and provide a more comprehensive understanding of therapy efficacy and safety. The benefits of increased access to investigational therapies extend beyond individual patients, contributing to the global advancement of healthcare and the reduction of health inequities.

Expertise

Harnessing global scientific expertise and infrastructure significantly enhances the conduct and quality of clinical studies, bringing numerous benefits to the research process. In an increasingly interconnected world, the opportunity to tap into a diverse array of scientific knowledge, cutting-edge technologies, and established research infrastructures across various countries has become a cornerstone of advancing clinical research. By integrating global expertise, researchers can leverage a broader spectrum of skills, perspectives, and methodologies, which can lead to more robust and innovative approaches to study design, execution, and data analysis.

One of the primary advantages of accessing global scientific expertise is the ability to collaborate with leading researchers and specialists from different fields and regions. This interdisciplinary approach allows for the incorporation of diverse scientific insights and methodologies, which can enhance the overall quality and depth of the research. For example, researchers working on complex medical conditions or novel therapies can benefit from the specialized knowledge of experts in various domains, such as genetics, pharmacology, or epidemiology, leading to more comprehensive and nuanced studies. This collaborative environment fosters the exchange of ideas and promotes the development of innovative solutions that might not emerge from a single research group or geographic location.

Global collaboration provides access to advanced research infrastructure and technologies that may not be available in every region. Institutions and research centers around the world often possess state-of-the-art equipment, laboratories, and facilities that can significantly improve the accuracy and efficiency of clinical trials. By partnering with these global entities, researchers can utilize the latest technologies for data collection, monitoring, and analysis, leading to higher-quality data and more reliable results. This access to cutting-edge infrastructure not only enhances the scientific rigor of the studies but also ensures that the research adheres to the highest standards of quality and safety.

The integration of global expertise also facilitates the adoption of best practices and standardization across clinical trials. Different countries and regions may have developed unique methodologies and approaches based on their own research experiences and regulatory requirements. By collaborating internationally, researchers can identify and implement the most effective practices from various contexts, leading to more consistent and standardized research protocols. This standardization is crucial for ensuring the comparability and reliability of study outcomes, particularly when trials involve multiple sites or are conducted across diverse populations.

In addition to improving study conduct and data quality, global collaboration enhances the ability to address complex research questions and explore novel therapeutic approaches. The pooling of resources and expertise allows researchers to undertake large-scale studies that may be beyond the scope of individual institutions or countries. This collaborative effort can accelerate the pace of discovery and innovation, leading to more rapid advancements in medical science and the development of new treatments. Furthermore, by involving a diverse range of scientific and clinical perspectives, researchers can better address the needs of varied patient populations and ensure that new therapies are applicable to a global audience.

Tapping into global scientific expertise and infrastructure offers substantial benefits for the conduct and quality of clinical research. By leveraging a wide array of knowledge, technologies, and best practices from around the world, researchers can enhance the rigor and efficiency of their studies, improve data quality, and accelerate the advancement of medical science. This global approach not only contributes to more effective and innovative research but also supports the development of treatments and solutions that are relevant and beneficial to diverse populations worldwide.

Challenges in Regulatory Harmonization

Regulatory harmonization presents a significant challenge in the globalization of clinical trials, as differences in regulatory requirements across countries can complicate and lengthen the approval processes. Each country has its own set of regulations and standards governing the conduct of clinical research, designed to ensure the safety and efficacy of investigational therapies while protecting patient rights. These regulations are shaped by local health policies, legal frameworks, and cultural considerations, leading to a diverse and sometimes fragmented landscape of regulatory requirements. Navigating this complexity requires careful coordination and a thorough understanding of the regulatory environments in multiple jurisdictions, which can pose substantial challenges for researchers and sponsors engaged in international trials.

One of the primary issues arising from regulatory diversity is the need to comply with varying submission and approval processes. Different countries may require distinct documentation, procedures, and timelines for obtaining regulatory approvals, which can lead to delays and increased costs. For instance, while one country might have streamlined procedures for fast-tracking innovative treatments, another might have more rigorous requirements for pre-market testing and safety assessments. These discrepancies necessitate additional resources and time for preparing and submitting the necessary documentation, as well as for addressing country-specific regulatory queries or modifications. This can significantly impact the overall timeline of a clinical trial, potentially delaying the availability of new treatments for patients and increasing the financial burden on sponsors.

Varying standards for data protection and patient consent add another layer of complexity. Each country has its own regulations concerning the handling of personal data and informed consent, which must be carefully adhered to in order to protect patient privacy and rights. For example, the General Data Protection Regulation (GDPR) in the European Union imposes stringent requirements on data handling and consent, which can differ from those in other regions. Ensuring compliance with these diverse data protection laws requires meticulous planning and coordination, as well as the implementation of robust data management systems to safeguard patient information across different jurisdictions.

Another challenge associated with regulatory harmonization is the need to adapt to differing requirements for trial design and reporting. Clinical trials conducted in multiple countries must often be tailored to meet the specific requirements of each regulatory authority, which can involve modifying study protocols, endpoints, or data collection methods. This can lead to inconsistencies in the study design and data interpretation, potentially affecting the validity and comparability of results across different regions. Additionally, discrepancies in reporting standards and practices can complicate the synthesis of trial findings and their subsequent use in regulatory submissions or public health decision-making.

Efforts towards regulatory harmonization aim to address these challenges by promoting greater alignment and cooperation among international regulatory bodies. Initiatives such as the International Council for Harmonization of Technical Requirements for Pharmaceuticals for Human Use (ICH) seek to establish common guidelines and standards for clinical research, facilitating more streamlined and efficient approval processes. By working towards greater regulatory consistency, these initiatives aim to reduce the burden on researchers and sponsors, accelerate the development of new therapies, and enhance the overall efficiency of global clinical trials.

Despite these efforts, achieving full regulatory harmonization remains a complex and ongoing process, requiring continued dialogue and collaboration among regulatory authorities, researchers, and industry stakeholders. In the meantime, navigating the diverse regulatory landscape requires a strategic approach, including thorough planning, robust documentation, and effective communication with regulatory bodies across different countries. By addressing these regulatory challenges and working towards greater alignment, the clinical research community can enhance the efficiency and effectiveness of global trials, ultimately leading to more timely and equitable access to innovative treatments for patients around the world.

Logistical Considerations

Conducting multinational clinical trials involves navigating a complex landscape of cultural, logistical, and language barriers, each of which poses distinct challenges to the successful execution and management of the study. These logistical considerations are crucial for ensuring that trials run smoothly and yield reliable, generalizable results across diverse populations.

Understanding and respecting cultural differences is fundamental to managing multinational trials. Cultural factors can influence various aspects of trial conduct, from participant recruitment and informed consent to adherence and response to treatment. For example, cultural beliefs and attitudes towards medical research and intervention can affect participants' willingness to enroll in a study or comply with its protocols. In some cultures, there may be a greater emphasis on traditional medicine or alternative therapies, which could impact participants' perceptions of and participation in clinical trials. Furthermore, cultural norms regarding health and communication can affect how patients interact with healthcare providers and researchers, potentially influencing the accuracy of reported outcomes. To address these cultural barriers, researchers must engage with local experts and community leaders to tailor recruitment strategies, consent processes, and intervention protocols to fit the cultural context of each region. Training study staff in cultural competence and sensitivity can also enhance their ability to build trust and rapport with participants from diverse backgrounds.

Coordinating the practical aspects of multinational trials presents a range of logistical challenges. These include managing the distribution of study materials, ensuring uniformity in data collection procedures, and coordinating the scheduling of study visits across different time zones. The complexity of logistics increases with the number of countries involved, as researchers must address differences in local infrastructure, healthcare systems, and regulatory requirements. For instance, the availability of medical facilities, equipment, and technology can vary significantly between countries, potentially affecting the consistency and quality of data collection. Additionally, managing the supply chain for investigational products, including ensuring proper storage and handling, requires careful planning and coordination to avoid delays or disruptions. Effective logistical management involves establishing clear communication channels, using advanced project management tools, and working closely with local partners to streamline operations and overcome regional challenges.

Language differences are a prominent logistical challenge in multinational trials. Communication issues can arise in various contexts, from obtaining informed consent and providing study instructions to collecting and interpreting data. Misunderstandings or inaccuracies in translation can lead to difficulties in ensuring that participants fully understand the study requirements and the potential risks and benefits. Additionally, language barriers can affect the quality of data collection and the ability to resolve issues promptly. To address these challenges, it is essential to provide study materials, including consent forms and questionnaires, in the native languages of the participating regions. Utilizing professional translation services and bilingual staff can help ensure that all communication is accurate and culturally appropriate. Training for research staff on language and communication strategies can also improve interactions with participants and facilitate more effective data collection.

Managing these barriers requires a well-coordinated approach that integrates cultural, logistical, and language considerations into the trial design and implementation processes. Developing a comprehensive project plan that outlines strategies for addressing these challenges and allocating resources accordingly can enhance the efficiency and effectiveness of multinational trials. Collaborating with local experts, utilizing technology to facilitate communication and data management, and maintaining a flexible and adaptive approach are key to overcoming these barriers and achieving successful trial outcomes.

By proactively addressing cultural, logistical, and language barriers, researchers can improve participant engagement, ensure consistent data quality, and enhance the overall success of multinational clinical trials. This careful and thoughtful approach helps to ensure that the trials are conducted ethically and effectively, ultimately leading to more robust and generalizable findings that can advance medical knowledge and improve patient care on a global scale.

Challenges in Clinical Research

Anticipating and addressing challenges in clinical research is crucial for preparing researchers and stakeholders for the evolving landscape of healthcare innovation. As clinical research continues to advance, several key areas require careful attention to ensure that future studies are both effective and equitable. This chapter delves into some of the most pressing challenges and emerging trends that will shape the future of clinical research, including diversity and inclusion, digital health technologies, artificial intelligence, regulatory changes, and globalization.

One of the foremost challenges in clinical research is ensuring diversity and inclusion in study populations. Including a broad range of participants based on demographics such as age, race, ethnicity, socioeconomic status, and geographic location is essential for generating results that are applicable to diverse patient groups. This approach not only enhances the generalizability of findings but also addresses health disparities by ensuring that investigational therapies are effective across various patient groups. Embracing diversity and inclusion helps to promote health equity and ensure that the benefits of clinical research are accessible to all.

The integration of digital health technologies into clinical research offers innovative solutions to streamline trial processes and enhance data collection and analysis. Remote monitoring through wearable devices and mobile health apps allows for real-time tracking of patient data, improving participant compliance and data accuracy. Digital health tools can also facilitate better patient engagement and more efficient data management, ultimately leading to more robust and insightful research outcomes.

AI plays a transformative role in clinical research by enabling predictive analytics to forecast patient outcomes, optimize trial design, and identify potential risks or adverse events. AI algorithms can analyze vast amounts of data quickly and accurately, providing valuable insights that inform decision-making and enhance the overall effectiveness of clinical trials. Additionally, AI-driven tools such as Natural Language Processing (NLP) help to extract meaningful insights from unstructured data, such as medical records and patient reports, further supporting evidence-based research and clinical practice.

Navigating the evolving regulatory landscape is essential for maintaining compliance and adapting to new standards in clinical research. Recent regulatory changes have introduced greater flexibility, such as the acceptance of real-world evidence (RWE) to support regulatory submissions and inform post-market surveillance. Additionally, adaptive trial designs now allow for mid-study modifications based on accumulating data, providing researchers with more opportunities to optimize trial outcomes. However, regulatory changes also require researchers to stay informed about new requirements and ensure that their practices align with updated guidelines.

The globalization of clinical trials promotes access to diverse patient populations and leverages global scientific expertise. Conducting trials across multiple countries can enhance the generalizability of findings and facilitate international collaboration. However, it also presents logistical and regulatory challenges, such as managing cultural differences, coordinating across different time zones, and addressing variations in regulatory requirements. Successful multinational trials require careful planning, effective communication, and collaboration with local experts to navigate these complexities.

Understanding and adapting to these challenges and trends is vital for advancing clinical research practices. By embracing diversity and inclusion, leveraging digital health technologies and AI, staying abreast of regulatory changes, and navigating the complexities of globalization, researchers can drive innovation and improve patient outcomes on a global scale. Addressing these dynamics will not only enhance the effectiveness of clinical research but also contribute to the development of more equitable and impactful healthcare solutions.

CHAPTER 8

Pathway to a Six-Figure Career in Clinical Research

Achieving a six-figure salary in clinical research demands a multifaceted approach involving advanced education, targeted career development, and the cultivation of specialized skills. First and foremost, a strong educational foundation is crucial; this typically involves obtaining a relevant bachelor's degree followed by a master's degree or higher in clinical research, public health, or a related field. Such advanced degrees not only provide a thorough understanding of clinical research methodologies and regulatory requirements but also distinguish candidates in a competitive job market.

Equally important is the strategic development of one's career through targeted experience and skill enhancement. Starting in entry-level roles such as Clinical Research Coordinator or Associate allows individuals to gain essential hands-on experience and demonstrate their capabilities. Progressing to senior roles, such as Project Manager or Director of Clinical Research, requires not only experience but also specialized skills in areas like trial design, data analysis, and regulatory compliance. Cultivating expertise in high-demand therapeutic areas and emerging technologies, such as digital health tools and artificial intelligence, can further enhance one's value. Networking with industry professionals, seeking mentorship, and staying abreast of industry trends contribute significantly to career advancement and can lead to lucrative opportunities. By integrating these elements—advanced education, strategic career moves, and continuous skill development—professionals in clinical research can successfully achieve a six-figure salary and thrive in this progressive field.

Consider these as you plan your career in clinical research.

1. Educational Foundation

- **Obtain Relevant Degrees:** Start with a solid educational foundation by earning a bachelor's degree in a related field such as life sciences, medicine, or public health. Follow this with a master's degree in clinical research, epidemiology, or a related discipline.
- **Pursue Advanced Certifications:** Enhance your qualifications with professional certifications such as Clinical Research Coordinator (CRC) or Clinical Research Associate (CRA) from recognized organizations like the Association of Clinical Research Professionals (ACRP) or the Society of Clinical Research Associates (SOCRA).

2. Gain Specialized Experience

- **Start with Entry-Level Positions:** Begin your career in roles such as Clinical Research Coordinator or Clinical Research Associate. Gain hands-on experience in managing trials, recruiting participants, and ensuring compliance with regulatory standards.
- **Advance to Senior Roles:** With experience, move into senior positions such as Project Manager, Clinical Operations Manager, or Director of Clinical Research. These roles involve overseeing multiple trials, managing teams, and contributing to strategic decision-making.

3. Develop Expertise and Skills

- **Specialize in High-Demand Areas:** Focus on high-demand therapeutic areas or specialized fields such as oncology, neurology, or rare diseases. Specialization can increase your value and earning potential.

- **Master Advanced Skills:** Acquire expertise in advanced areas such as data analytics, regulatory compliance, and clinical trial design. Familiarize yourself with emerging technologies and trends like digital health tools and artificial intelligence.

4. Expand Professional Network

- **Build a Strong Professional Network:** Join professional organizations, attend industry conferences, and participate in networking events. Building relationships with industry experts and peers can lead to career advancement opportunities and higher salaries.

- **Seek Mentorship:** Find mentors who can provide guidance, share industry insights, and help you navigate your career path.

5. Demonstrate Leadership and Innovation

- **Lead Successful Projects:** Take on leadership roles in high-profile projects or innovative research studies, and even volunteer at organizations to serve on committees or boards. Demonstrating your ability to manage complex trials and deliver successful outcomes can position you for higher-level positions and increased compensation.

- **Contribute to Publications and Presentations:** Publish research findings in peer-reviewed journals and present at conferences. Building a strong professional reputation through research contributions can enhance your career prospects.

6. Negotiate Salary and Career Advancement

- **Negotiate Your Salary:** When offered new positions or promotions, negotiate your salary and benefits. Research industry salary standards and be prepared to articulate your value based on your experience, skills, and contributions.

- **Seek Career Advancement Opportunities:** Continuously look for opportunities to advance your career, whether through promotions, lateral moves to different organizations, or pursuing executive roles within clinical research organizations.

By following this pathway, you can strategically position yourself for a lucrative career in clinical research. Combining advanced education, specialized skills, leadership, and effective networking will help you achieve a six-figure salary and excel in this dynamic and rewarding field.

Sample Educational Foundation and Pathway

```
├── Obtain Relevant Degrees
│       ├── Bachelor's Degree in Life Sciences, Medicine, Public Health
│       └── Master's Degree in Clinical Research, Epidemiology, Related Discipline
└── Pursue Advanced Certifications
        ├── Clinical Research Coordinator (CRC)
        └── Clinical Research Associate (CRA)

Gain Specialized Experience
├── Start with Entry-Level Positions
│       ├── Clinical Research Coordinator
│       └── Clinical Research Associate
└── Advance to Senior Roles
        ├── Project Manager
        ├── Clinical Operations Manager
        └── Director of Clinical Research

Develop Expertise and Skills
├── Specialize in High-Demand Areas
│       ├── Oncology
│       ├── Neurology
│       └── Rare Diseases
└── Master Advanced Skills
        ├── Data Analytics
        ├── Regulatory Compliance
        ├── Clinical Trial Design
        └── Emerging Technologies (Digital Health, AI)

Expand Professional Network
├── Build a Strong Professional Network
│       ├── Join Professional Organizations
│       └── Attend Industry Conferences and Networking Events
└── Seek Mentorship
        ├── Find Mentors for Guidance
        └── Gain Industry Insights

Demonstrate Leadership and Innovation
├── Lead Successful Projects
│       ├── High-Profile Projects
│       └── Volunteering for Committees or Boards
└── Contribute to Publications and Presentations
        ├── Publish Research Findings
        └── Present at Conferences

Negotiate Salary and Career Advancement
├── Negotiate Your Salary
│       ├── Research Industry Salary Standards
│       └── Articulate Your Value
└── Seek Career Advancement Opportunities
        ├── Promotions
        ├── Lateral Moves
        └── Executive Roles
```

CHAPTER 9

Crafting Your Professional Image in Clinical Research

The Power of a Cover Letter

A compelling cover letter is a pivotal element of your job application in clinical research, as it acts as your initial introduction to potential employers. It provides a unique opportunity to convey your enthusiasm for the role and demonstrate why you are a strong fit for the position. Crafting a tailored cover letter requires attention to detail and personalization. Start by addressing the hiring manager by name, if possible, which adds a personal touch and shows that you have done your research about the organization. Clearly state the position you are applying for and express your genuine interest in the role.

In the body of the cover letter, delve into how your educational background and professional experience align with the job requirements. Highlight specific examples from your previous roles that showcase your expertise in clinical research. For instance, if the job requires experience with managing clinical trials, mention a relevant project where you successfully oversaw multiple aspects of the trial, including participant recruitment and data analysis. Emphasize your skills in areas like regulatory compliance or data management, and provide concrete examples of how these skills have contributed to successful research outcomes.

Your cover letter should reflect an understanding of the organization's mission and how your values and career goals align with theirs. This demonstrates that you are not only seeking a job but are genuinely interested in contributing to the organization's objectives. Conclude with a strong closing statement that reiterates your enthusiasm for the position and your readiness to bring your skills and experience to the role. Express a desire for a follow-up discussion or interview, highlighting your eagerness to explore how you can contribute to the organization's success. This final touch reinforces your commitment and positions you as a proactive and motivated candidate.

Sample Cover Letter

[Your Name]
[Your Address]
[City, State, ZIP]
[Email Address]
[Phone Number]
[Date]

[Hiring Manager's Name]
[Company Name]
[Company Address]
[City, State, ZIP]

Dear [Hiring Manager's Name],

I am excited to apply for the [Position Title] position at [Company Name], as advertised. With a strong background in clinical research and a deep commitment to advancing health equity, I am eager to contribute my skills in trial coordination, regulatory compliance, and participant engagement to your team. I believe my blend of hands-on research experience and passion for inclusive, ethical research practices aligns well with your mission.

Over the course of my career, I have successfully managed clinical trials across multiple phases, ensuring adherence to GCP guidelines while maintaining high standards of participant care and data integrity. I have experience with IRB submissions, site monitoring, patient recruitment, and collaborating across multidisciplinary teams. Additionally, I am adept at navigating the complexities of clinical trial operations while fostering trusting relationships with diverse communities—an essential skill for driving participant enrollment and retention.

I am enthusiastic about the opportunity to bring my experience to [Company Name] and support your innovative research efforts. I would welcome the chance to discuss how my background aligns with your needs and how I can add value to your team.

Thank you for considering my application. I look forward to the possibility of contributing to your important work.

Sincerely,
[Your Name]

Résumé Components for Clinical Research

A well-structured résumé is essential in clinical research to effectively communicate your qualifications and experiences. Utilize a clear and professional résumé template that highlights key sections: Contact Information, Professional Summary, Skills, Work Experience, Education, and Certifications.

Provide contact information. Include your full name, phone number, email address, and LinkedIn profile, if applicable. You may also want to include a professional headshot.

You will also need a professional summary. A well-crafted professional summary is an essential component of your résumé, as it provides a succinct overview of your career goals, key skills, and unique qualifications. This summary should capture the essence of your professional identity, particularly highlighting your expertise in clinical research and any areas of specialization. Start by briefly outlining your career objectives, ensuring they align with the position you are seeking. For example, if you are targeting a role in clinical trials management, your summary could emphasize your commitment to advancing research methodologies and improving patient outcomes.

Incorporate a clear and focused description of your key skills, particularly those that are relevant to clinical research. Highlight your proficiency in areas such as data analysis, regulatory compliance, trial design, and participant management. Mention any specific techniques or tools you are adept at, such as statistical software or electronic data capture systems, to illustrate your technical capabilities. Additionally, if you have experience with emerging technologies or methodologies, such as digital health tools or adaptive trial designs, include these to showcase your forward-thinking approach and adaptability.

Convey what you bring to the table by summarizing your notable achievements and contributions in the field. This might include successful management of high-profile research projects, innovative solutions to complex research problems, or significant improvements in trial efficiency or data accuracy. A strong professional summary should not only reflect your past accomplishments but also convey how your skills and experience will benefit the potential employer. By presenting a clear and compelling snapshot of your qualifications and career goals, you set a strong foundation for the rest of your résumé and make a powerful impression on prospective employers.

Always highlight your skills. When outlining your skills in clinical research, it's essential to provide a comprehensive overview that highlights your proficiency in key areas critical to the field. Start by emphasizing your expertise in trial management, which involves coordinating various aspects of clinical trials, including site selection, patient recruitment, and monitoring. Detail your ability to manage trial timelines, ensure adherence to protocols, and facilitate communication among team members, all of which are crucial for the successful execution of research studies.

Next, underscore your skills in data analysis, which are fundamental to interpreting research results and drawing meaningful conclusions. Highlight your proficiency in analyzing complex datasets, performing statistical evaluations, and using specialized software to generate reports and visualize data. This demonstrates your capability to handle large volumes of information accurately and extract insights that drive clinical decision-making.

Regulatory compliance is another critical area to address, as adhering to regulatory standards ensures the integrity of the research and the safety of participants. Illustrate your knowledge of relevant regulations and guidelines, such as Good Clinical Practice (GCP), and your experience in preparing for audits, managing documentation, and implementing corrective actions as needed.

Finally, showcase your proficiency with Clinical Trial Management Systems (CTMS), which are essential for organizing and managing trial data and processes. Mention specific CTMS platforms you are familiar with, and describe how your skills with these systems enhance your ability to track trial progress, manage documentation, and ensure data accuracy. By presenting a well-rounded skill set that encompasses trial management, data analysis, regulatory compliance, and CTMS proficiency, you demonstrate your comprehensive expertise and readiness to contribute effectively to any clinical research team.

Sample Résumé

[Your Full Name]
[Your City, State ZIP]
[Your Email Address] • [Your Phone Number] • [LinkedIn URL]

<u>Professional Summary</u>

Detail-oriented and certified Clinical Research Professional with [X] years of experience coordinating clinical trials across Phases I–IV. Skilled in regulatory compliance, patient recruitment, informed consent, and data management with a strong commitment to Good Clinical Practice (GCP) and ethical standards. Adept at collaborating with cross-functional teams to ensure study milestones are met on time and within budget. Passionate about advancing diversity in clinical trials and delivering high-quality, patient-centered research.

<u>Core Competencies</u>

Clinical Trial Coordination (Phases I–IV)
Regulatory Submissions (IRB, FDA)
Informed Consent & Patient Recruitment
Good Clinical Practice (GCP) Compliance
Electronic Data Capture (EDC) Systems (e.g., REDCap, Medidata)
Site Monitoring & Query Resolution
Adverse Event Reporting (SAEs, AEs)
Diversity & Inclusion in Clinical Research

<u>Professional Experience</u>

Clinical Research Coordinator
[Institution or Company Name], [City, State]
[Month, Year] – Present

- Coordinated multiple clinical trials from start-up to close-out in therapeutic areas such as oncology, cardiology, and infectious disease.
- Screened, recruited, and consented study participants, ensuring adherence to protocol and ethical standards.
- Managed regulatory documents, including IRB submissions, protocol amendments, and continuing reviews.
- Collected, entered, and validated clinical data in EDC systems, maintaining a 98% query resolution rate.
- Liaised with sponsors, CROs, and monitors during site visits, audits, and interim monitoring visits.
- Facilitated diversity-focused recruitment initiatives, increasing enrollment of underrepresented populations by 20%.

Clinical Research Assistant

[Institution or Company Name], [City, State]
[Month, Year] – [Month, Year]

- Supported coordination of investigator-initiated and industry-sponsored trials.
- Prepared source documents and maintained participant study files in compliance with SOPs.
- Scheduled patient visits and study assessments in collaboration with clinical care teams.
- Assisted with safety reporting and tracking of adverse events.
- Conducted data entry and resolved data queries in REDCap and Medidata Rave.

Education

Master of Science (MS), Clinical Research
[University Name], [City, State]

[Month, Year]

Bachelor of Science (BS), [Your Major]
[University Name], [City, State]
[Month, Year]

Certifications

Certified Clinical Research Coordinator (CCRC) – ACRP, [Year]
Good Clinical Practice (GCP) Certification – [Training Provider], [Year]
Human Subjects Protection (HSP) Certification – [Provider], [Year]

Technical Skills

EDC Systems: REDCap, Medidata Rave, Oracle InForm
CTMS: [Clinical Trial Management Systems you've used]
Microsoft Office Suite (Excel, Word, PowerPoint)
eRegulatory Systems: Florence, Veeva Vault

Professional Affiliations

Association of Clinical Research Professionals (ACRP)
Society for Clinical Research Sites (SCRS)

Volunteer or Community Involvement

(Optional but powerful, especially if it aligns with health equity or research)
Volunteer Research Recruiter, [Organization]
Health Educator, [Community Program]

Work Experience

When detailing your work experience on your résumé or CV, it's crucial to present it in reverse chronological order, starting with your most recent position and working backward. This format allows potential employers to see your most current and relevant roles first, highlighting your career progression and the latest skills you've acquired.

Begin each entry with your job title, followed by the name of the employer and the dates of your employment. This provides a clear context for your role within each organization. For example, "Clinical Research Coordinator, XYZ Research Institute, January 2021 – Present."

In describing each position, focus on your responsibilities and accomplishments, making sure to use action verbs to convey your contributions effectively. Start with verbs like "managed," "developed," "coordinated," or "implemented" to demonstrate your active involvement and leadership in the role. For instance, you might write, "Managed a team of 5 research associates in the execution of a multi-site clinical trial, ensuring adherence to protocol and regulatory requirements."

Include quantifiable results to provide concrete evidence of your achievements. For example, "Oversaw the recruitment and enrollment of 300+ participants for a phase III oncology trial, resulting in a 20% increase in participant retention compared to previous studies." This approach not only highlights your capabilities but also shows the tangible impact of your work.

Additionally, describe any specific projects or initiatives you led or contributed to, emphasizing how they aligned with the organization's goals or improved processes. For instance, "Developed a new data management system that reduced data entry errors by 15% and streamlined the reporting process, enhancing overall trial efficiency."

By detailing your work experience in this structured and results-oriented manner, you effectively communicate your expertise, demonstrate your impact in previous roles, and showcase your suitability for future positions in the field of clinical research.

Education and Certifications: When detailing your educational background and certifications on your résumé or CV, it's essential to provide a clear and structured overview that highlights your qualifications and demonstrates your expertise in clinical research.

Start with your highest degree and work backward. List the degree earned, the institution from which it was obtained, and the year of graduation. For example, "Master of Science in Clinical Research, Mount Sinai School of Medicine, 2018." If applicable, include any honors or distinctions received, such as "Graduated with Distinction" or "Summa Cum Laude." For relevant degrees, you might also want to highlight specific coursework or research projects that are pertinent to clinical research, such as "Completed a thesis on clinical trial design and analysis."

If you have additional degrees or certifications that contribute to your qualifications in clinical research, list them in descending order of relevance. For example, "Bachelor of Science in Biology, University of California, 2016," followed by any relevant coursework or special projects.

Certifications are critical in demonstrating your specialized knowledge and skills in clinical research. Start with the most relevant certifications, providing the name of the certification, the issuing organization, and the date obtained. For instance, "Certified Clinical Research Coordinator (CRC), Association of Clinical Research Professionals (ACRP), 2020" or "Certified Clinical Research Associate (CRA), Society of Clinical Research Associates (SOCRA), 2019."

If you have multiple certifications, list them in order of relevance to the position you're applying for, and consider including any ongoing professional development or continuing education courses. For example, "Completed Advanced Training in GCP (Good Clinical Practice) and Data Management, 2021."

Be sure to include any certifications that demonstrate your commitment to staying current with industry standards and regulations, as these show your dedication to maintaining high professional standards and your readiness to adapt to evolving practices in clinical research. By presenting your educational background and certifications clearly and comprehensively, you provide a strong foundation for your qualifications, showcasing your preparedness for advanced roles in clinical research and reinforcing your credibility as a professional in the field.

Professional Affiliations

Professional affiliations are a vital aspect of building and advancing your career in clinical research. Membership in relevant professional organizations and societies not only provides access to a wealth of resources and networking opportunities but also enhances your credibility and visibility within the field.

Begin by listing memberships in key organizations that are relevant to clinical research, such as the Association of Clinical Research Professionals (ACRP), the Society of Clinical Research Associates (SOCRA), or the Drug Information Association (DIA). For example, you might write, "Member, Association of Clinical Research Professionals (ACRP), since 2018" or "Active Member, Society of Clinical Research Associates (SOCRA), since 2020." Including the dates of membership can further demonstrate your commitment to staying engaged with the industry.

Volunteering for committees within these professional organizations offers numerous benefits that can significantly enhance your career. By participating in committees, you have the opportunity to influence industry practices, contribute to the development of guidelines and standards, and gain exposure to influential professionals and thought leaders. For instance, serving on a committee focused on clinical trial standards or regulatory affairs allows you to stay at the forefront of emerging trends and contribute to shaping best practices. Volunteering for committees also provides valuable experience in leadership and project management, skills that are highly regarded in clinical research roles. It can also open doors to new professional relationships and mentorship opportunities, offering insights into different career paths and advancement strategies.

Engaging with professional organizations and volunteering can lead to enhanced career prospects in several ways. It can increase your visibility in the field, making you a more attractive candidate for advanced positions or specialized roles. It also provides opportunities to collaborate on innovative projects and research, which can enhance your résumé and professional reputation. Additionally, being an active member of professional societies can lead to invitations to speak at conferences, publish in industry journals, and participate in cutting-edge research initiatives.

Active participation in professional affiliations and volunteering for committees not only enriches your professional network but also positions you as a leader and expert in the field of clinical research. These activities demonstrate your commitment to the industry, provide valuable experience, and can significantly advance your career by keeping you engaged with the latest developments and opportunities in clinical research.

Navigating the Interview Process

The interview process for clinical research positions is a crucial step where you have the chance to showcase your skills, experience, and fit for the role. Preparation is essential to make a strong impression. Begin by researching the organization extensively. Understand its mission, values, and recent projects or breakthroughs. This knowledge will help you tailor your responses to align with the organization's goals and demonstrate your genuine interest in their work. Review the job description carefully to identify key responsibilities and required skills, and reflect on how your background matches these needs. Prepare for common interview questions related to clinical research, such as those focused on trial management, data handling, and regulatory compliance. Practice articulating your experiences and accomplishments in these areas, using specific examples to highlight your expertise and problem-solving abilities.

During the interview, communicate clearly and confidently. Highlight specific examples of your work that demonstrate your abilities and achievements. Be prepared to discuss how you approach challenges in clinical research and how you stay current with industry trends and regulations. Ask thoughtful questions about the role, team dynamics, and the organization's research focus. Effective communication is pivotal during the interview process. When discussing your qualifications, be clear, concise, and confident. Use specific examples to illustrate your achievements and how they relate to the responsibilities of the position. For instance, if asked about your experience with trial management, describe a project where you successfully managed multiple aspects of a clinical trial, highlighting any challenges you overcame and the impact of your work. Demonstrate your ability to handle complex data by discussing how you ensured accuracy and integrity in previous roles.

Addressing regulatory compliance, share examples of how you navigated regulatory requirements and ensured adherence to guidelines. Communicate your problem-solving strategies and how you stay updated with industry trends and regulations. This will showcase your proactive approach and commitment to the field.

During the interview, it is important to engage thoughtfully with the questions posed. When discussing challenges you have faced in clinical research, focus on your problem-solving approach and the outcomes achieved. Explain how you address issues such as participant recruitment, data discrepancies, or regulatory hurdles. Demonstrate your ability to stay current with industry developments by discussing recent advancements or trends and how they might influence clinical research practices. Asking insightful questions about the role, team dynamics, and the organization's research focus shows your interest in the position and helps you assess if the organization aligns with your career goals. Inquire about the team's approach to collaboration, the organization's strategic priorities, and opportunities for professional growth within the company.

After the interview, send a thank-you note to express your appreciation for the opportunity to interview. Reiterate your interest in the position and briefly mention a key point from the interview that reinforces your fit for the role. Reflect on the interview experience to identify areas where you performed well and aspects that could be improved for future interviews. Consider how you can further align your skills and experiences with the needs of potential employers. This reflection will not only help you improve your interview skills but also prepare you for subsequent opportunities in the field of clinical research.

By thoroughly preparing, communicating effectively, engaging thoughtfully with interview questions, and reflecting on your performance, you position yourself as a strong candidate for clinical research roles. This approach will enhance your chances of securing a position that aligns with your career goals and aspirations.

Professionalism and etiquette are fundamental components of a successful interview process and play a significant role in creating a positive impression on potential employers. Dressing appropriately is one of the first steps to demonstrating your professionalism. Choose business attire that reflects the standards of the industry and the specific organization you are interviewing with. A well-tailored suit, clean and polished shoes, and a neat hairstyle contribute to a polished appearance and convey respect for the interview process.

Arriving on time is crucial to setting a positive tone for the interview. Aim to arrive 10–15 minutes early to account for any unforeseen delays and to give yourself a moment to settle in before the interview begins. Punctuality not only demonstrates your respect for the interviewer's time but also reflects your organizational skills and reliability. Once you arrive, be polite and respectful to everyone you encounter, from the receptionist to other staff members. Your interactions with these individuals can be part of the overall evaluation process, so maintaining a courteous demeanor throughout is essential.

During the interview itself, maintaining good eye contact is important as it conveys confidence and attentiveness. Actively listen to the questions and responses, and avoid interrupting the interviewer. This shows that you value their input and are engaged in the conversation. Demonstrating enthusiasm and a positive attitude throughout the interview helps create a memorable and favorable impression. Your energy and eagerness to contribute to the organization can significantly impact how you are perceived.

Following up after the interview is a critical step in reinforcing your interest in the position and leaving a lasting positive impression. Send a thank-you email within 24 hours of the interview, expressing your appreciation for the opportunity to discuss the role. In your email, briefly mention a key point from the interview that resonated with you and reiterate your enthusiasm for the position. This follow-up not only shows your appreciation but also reinforces your suitability for the role and keeps you top of mind for the hiring team.

By adhering to these etiquette principles, you demonstrate professionalism, respect, and enthusiasm—qualities that are highly valued in any clinical research role. These practices can greatly enhance your chances of making a positive impression and securing the position you desire.

Crafting a tailored cover letter, utilizing a clear résumé template, and adhering to interview best practices are crucial steps in enhancing your chances of securing a desired role in clinical research. A well-tailored cover letter allows you to directly address the specific needs and values of the organization, showcasing your relevant skills and enthusiasm for the position. By personalizing your cover letter to highlight how your background aligns with the job requirements, you demonstrate your genuine interest and suitability for the role. Meanwhile, using a clear and professionally designed résumé template ensures that your qualifications are presented in an organized and visually appealing manner, making it easier for hiring managers to quickly assess your experience and skills.

In addition, adhering to interview best practices, such as thorough preparation, demonstrating professionalism, and following up with a thank-you note, further strengthens your candidacy. Always ensure that your answers are truthful and accurate. Effective preparation allows you to discuss your expertise and experience confidently, while professionalism during the interview process reflects your respect for the opportunity and your potential fit within the organization. By integrating these strategies, you not only improve your chances of securing an interview but also position yourself as a strong candidate who is well-prepared and committed to advancing your career in clinical research.

Sample Interview Questions and Potential Answers

1. Tell me about yourself and what interests you about clinical research.

Sample Answer: I have a background in [public health/health sciences] and developed a strong interest in clinical research because I want to be part of advancing new treatments and improving patient outcomes. I'm especially passionate about ensuring diverse populations are represented in trials, which I believe is essential for equitable healthcare. Through my academic training and hands-on experience supporting research projects, I've gained skills in patient coordination, data collection, and compliance—and I'm excited to grow further in this field.

2. What is Good Clinical Practice (GCP), and why is it important?

Sample Answer: Good Clinical Practice is an international ethical and scientific quality standard for designing, conducting, recording, and reporting clinical trials. It ensures that the rights, safety, and well-being of trial participants are protected and that the trial data are credible. Following GCP is critical because it builds trust with participants and ensures that research can be used to make important healthcare decisions.

3. How do you handle working with diverse patient populations?

Sample Answer: I believe diversity in clinical trials is essential. I approach every participant with cultural sensitivity and respect, making sure they fully understand the study and feel comfortable asking questions. In my past role, I worked on outreach efforts to engage underrepresented communities, which included adjusting communication methods and addressing barriers like transportation or mistrust. Building rapport is key.

4. Describe your experience with informed consent.

Sample Answer: Informed consent is a vital part of ethical research. While I have supported the process by preparing consent forms and helping answer participant questions, I understand that it's not just about getting a signature. It's about ensuring the participant truly understands the study, its risks, benefits, and their rights. I make sure the process is thorough and that participants know they can withdraw at any time without penalty.

5. How do you manage multiple tasks or prioritize when things get busy?

Sample Answer: In clinical research, I know it's common to juggle participant visits, data entry, and regulatory tasks at the same time. I prioritize by focusing on participant safety and visit schedules first, then managing data entry and documentation in order of deadlines. I also keep detailed to-do lists and use calendars or trackers to stay organized, ensuring nothing falls through the cracks.

6. Tell me about a time you noticed an error or discrepancy. How did you handle it?

Sample Answer: In one study, I noticed that a participant's date of birth was recorded incorrectly in the database. I double-checked the source document, confirmed the correct information, and reported the discrepancy to the study coordinator. We corrected the entry and filed a data clarification note, following the protocol. I believe attention to detail and prompt reporting are crucial in research.

7. Why do you want to work at our site/company?

Sample Answer: I'm drawn to your site because of your reputation for conducting diverse and impactful clinical trials. I noticed you have a focus on [mention a specific disease area or diversity initiative if known], and I would love to contribute my skills while learning from your experienced team. Your commitment to both scientific excellence and patient care aligns with my own values.

8. Where do you see yourself in 3–5 years in clinical research?

Sample Answer: In the next few years, I hope to become a seasoned Clinical Research Coordinator or even move toward a CRA role, gaining experience with monitoring and multi-site trials. Long-term, I'm interested in contributing to diversity initiatives and possibly mentoring newer research professionals. I'm committed to growing within the field and staying current with regulations and best practices.

CHAPTER 10

Your Potential Impact in Clinical Research

If it's your calling and passion, go on and make an impact with your career in clinical research. Embracing the opportunities and challenges in clinical research positions you at the forefront of medical innovation, where each decision and discovery has the potential to transform lives. As you navigate your career in this dynamic field, you become an integral part of a larger mission to advance medical science and enhance patient care. Clinical research is not merely a profession but a profound commitment to understanding and addressing the complexities of human health. By tackling the diverse and evolving challenges—from designing robust studies to interpreting complex data—you are actively shaping the future of medicine and ensuring that new therapies are both effective and equitable.

Mastering clinical research goes beyond achieving professional milestones; it involves contributing to a global effort to improve health outcomes and drive progress. Each study you undertake, every protocol you refine, and each patient you engage with brings us closer to breakthroughs that can alleviate suffering and save lives. Your work has the potential to influence treatment paradigms, inform public health policies, and foster innovations that can address unmet medical needs worldwide. As you advance in your career, remember that your dedication not only advances your professional journey but also plays a critical role in creating a healthier, more informed world.

Embracing the opportunities and challenges in clinical research presents a unique and dynamic environment where the realms of scientific discovery and patient care intersect. This field offers a platform to explore new treatments, enhance understanding of diseases, and ultimately, contribute to significant improvements in global health. By tackling challenges such as ensuring diversity in clinical trials, you can help ensure that findings are applicable to a broad spectrum of populations, thereby increasing the generalizability and impact of research outcomes. Integrating digital health technologies and artificial intelligence further revolutionizes this landscape, enabling more precise data collection, real-time monitoring, and sophisticated data analysis, which can lead to more personalized and effective treatments.

Navigating regulatory changes is another critical aspect of clinical research that requires adaptability and foresight. Keeping abreast of evolving regulations ensures compliance while optimizing the design and execution of clinical trials. Additionally, embracing globalization allows researchers to access diverse patient populations and expertise from around the world, enriching the research process and facilitating international collaboration. This comprehensive approach not only drives scientific innovation but also enhances patient care by ensuring that new treatments are safe, effective, and accessible to diverse populations. Through these efforts, you can contribute to advancing medical knowledge and improving patient outcomes on a global scale, making a meaningful impact in the field of healthcare.

Contributing to medical innovation in clinical research transcends the fundamental tasks of protocol development and data analysis, embodying a profound role in shaping the future of healthcare. At the core of this endeavor is collaboration with a diverse array of stakeholders, including patients, healthcare professionals, regulatory agencies, and academic institutions. This collaborative approach ensures that research is grounded in real-world needs and perspectives, leading to the development of therapies that address a wide range of health conditions and improve overall patient outcomes. By working together with these stakeholders, researchers can integrate diverse insights and expertise, fostering innovations that are both impactful and relevant to various patient populations.

Leveraging cutting-edge technologies is another crucial aspect of contributing to medical innovation. The integration of advanced digital health technologies and artificial intelligence into clinical research enhances the precision and efficiency of data collection and analysis. Wearable devices and mobile health applications provide real-time monitoring of patient health, while AI algorithms offer sophisticated predictive analytics to anticipate patient outcomes and optimize trial designs. These technological advancements facilitate more accurate and timely insights, enabling researchers to refine therapies and adapt interventions based on emerging data. As a result, new treatments can be developed more rapidly and tailored more effectively to meet the needs of diverse patient populations.

Adhering to rigorous ethical standards is essential in ensuring that clinical research is conducted with integrity and respect for patient rights. Ethical considerations encompass obtaining informed consent, safeguarding patient confidentiality, and ensuring the safety and well-being of participants throughout the research process. By maintaining high ethical standards, researchers not only uphold the trust of patients but also contribute to the credibility and validity of the research findings. This commitment to ethics helps ensure that new therapies are not only innovative but also safe and equitable, thereby enhancing their acceptance and integration into clinical practice.

Furthermore, contributing to medical innovation involves a continuous process of learning and adaptation. The field of clinical research is dynamic, with new discoveries, technologies, and regulatory changes constantly shaping its landscape. Staying abreast of these developments and embracing a mindset of continuous improvement allows researchers to remain at the forefront of innovation. By adapting to new methodologies, exploring emerging research areas, and refining existing practices, researchers can drive progress and contribute to the advancement of medical science.

Ultimately, your role in clinical research is integral to developing new therapies, improving treatment efficacy, and enhancing healthcare accessibility. By embracing collaboration, leveraging advanced technologies, adhering to ethical standards, and remaining adaptable, you play a vital part in shaping the future of healthcare. This comprehensive approach ensures that research efforts translate into meaningful improvements in patient care and contribute to the broader goal of advancing global health.

Making a lasting impact in clinical research involves more than just achieving technical milestones; it encompasses the broader vision of transforming lives through every advancement, from innovative trial designs to breakthrough treatments. Each successful trial and new therapy represents a significant leap forward in our understanding of diseases and the development of effective interventions. These advancements have the potential to dramatically improve patient outcomes, offering hope and tangible benefits to individuals suffering from previously untreatable conditions. By dedicating yourself to excellence in research, you play a crucial role in translating scientific discoveries into real-world solutions that enhance quality of life and extend healthy lifespans.

Commitment to continuous learning is a cornerstone of making a lasting impact. The field of clinical research is ever-evolving, with new technologies, methodologies, and scientific discoveries constantly reshaping the landscape. Staying current with these developments ensures that you are applying the most advanced and effective techniques in your research. It also involves actively seeking out new knowledge and refining your skills to meet the demands of a rapidly changing field. By embracing ongoing education and professional growth, you contribute to a culture of innovation and progress that drives the field forward and maximizes the impact of your work.

Ethical conduct is integral to maintaining the integrity of scientific inquiry and inspiring confidence in research outcomes. Upholding rigorous ethical standards—such as ensuring informed consent, safeguarding participant confidentiality, and conducting research with transparency—builds trust with patients, stakeholders, and the public. This ethical foundation is essential for the credibility of research findings and the successful implementation of new therapies. By demonstrating an unwavering commitment to ethical practices, you help ensure that research advances are both scientifically valid and socially responsible, thereby reinforcing the value of clinical research in improving patient care and outcomes.

Ultimately, the impact of clinical research extends beyond the laboratory and trial settings. Each breakthrough and advancement contributes to a larger narrative of progress in medicine, with the potential to effect meaningful change on a global scale. By dedicating yourself to excellence, embracing continuous learning, and adhering to ethical standards, you not only advance the field but also contribute to a legacy of innovation that benefits countless individuals. This holistic approach ensures that your work in clinical research leaves a lasting mark on both the scientific community and the lives of those who benefit from new and improved treatments.

Looking ahead in the field of clinical research requires a proactive approach to staying informed and adaptable. The landscape of clinical research is continuously evolving, driven by rapid advancements in technology, shifting regulatory frameworks, and emerging trends in healthcare. To remain at the forefront of this dynamic field, it is essential to keep abreast of the latest developments and integrate new knowledge into your practice. This involves regularly reviewing current literature, participating in industry conferences, and engaging with professional networks to stay updated on cutting-edge research methods and regulatory changes.

Embracing technological innovations is a key component of adapting to the evolving landscape. Digital health technologies, artificial intelligence, and other emerging tools are transforming how clinical trials are designed, conducted, and analyzed. Familiarity with these advancements not only enhances your research capabilities but also positions you to leverage new technologies for more efficient and effective trials. By understanding and utilizing these tools, you can improve data accuracy, streamline processes, and contribute to the development of novel therapies with greater precision.

Cultivating a mindset of adaptability and resilience is crucial for navigating the inherent challenges in clinical research. The field is characterized by its complexity and the need to respond to unforeseen issues, such as evolving patient needs, regulatory hurdles, or technological glitches. Being adaptable means embracing change and continuously seeking ways to improve your practices in response to these challenges. Resilience, on the other hand, involves maintaining a positive and solution-oriented attitude in the face of setbacks, ensuring that you remain focused on achieving your research goals despite obstacles.

Professional growth and development are integral to a successful career in clinical research. This includes pursuing ongoing education, seeking mentorship, and exploring opportunities for advancement within the field. By actively engaging in professional development, you can enhance your skills, expand your expertise, and position yourself for leadership roles. Staying open to new learning opportunities and career paths not only enriches your personal and professional growth but also contributes to the advancement of the field as a whole.

In summary, looking ahead in clinical research involves a commitment to staying informed about emerging trends and innovations, embracing technological advancements, and cultivating adaptability and resilience. By proactively addressing these aspects, you can navigate the evolving landscape of clinical research with confidence, drive your professional development, and contribute meaningfully to the advancement of healthcare and patient outcomes.

Mastering clinical research is a profound and transformative journey that intertwines discovery, innovation, and responsibility. This journey is not merely about following established protocols and methodologies but involves a deep commitment to advancing the frontiers of medical science and improving patient outcomes. Each step in clinical research—from designing trials to analyzing data and interpreting results—requires a blend of meticulous attention to detail, creative problem-solving, and ethical integrity. Embracing this journey with dedication and passion means not only achieving personal career milestones but also contributing significantly to the collective effort of enhancing global health.

As you advance in clinical research, your role becomes central to shaping the future of medicine. The discoveries and innovations you contribute have the potential to revolutionize treatment paradigms, introduce novel therapies, and address unmet medical needs. This transformative impact extends beyond the laboratory and clinical settings, influencing the broader healthcare landscape and improving patient care on a global scale. By diligently applying your expertise and staying abreast of emerging trends and technologies, you play a crucial role in driving forward the boundaries of scientific knowledge and clinical practice.

Your efforts in clinical research are pivotal to advancing science and enhancing patient care. The challenges and breakthroughs you encounter are integral to the progress of medical research and the development of new treatment options. Each study you conduct, each trial you manage, and each patient outcome you impact contributes to a larger narrative of progress and improvement in healthcare. Your work not only furthers scientific understanding but also has a direct and meaningful effect on the well-being of individuals and communities around the world.

Ultimately, the journey of mastering clinical research is about leaving a lasting legacy in global health. The advancements you contribute to and the knowledge you generate help pave the way for future research and innovation. By committing to excellence in your work, you ensure that your efforts make a positive and enduring impact on the health and well-being of people everywhere. Your dedication to clinical research is a testament to your role as a vital contributor to the ongoing evolution of medicine and the quest to improve global health outcomes.

Closing Thoughts

Your pathway to success starts now. As we come to the close of this book, I want to leave you with a powerful truth: Success in clinical research is possible for you. I know this because I started exactly where many of you may be today. I started at the entry level. I learned the ropes. I faced the doubts and wondered how far I could really go. Over time, through hard work, determination, and a commitment to growth, I advanced from those early roles to become a director of clinical trials, and now, I have the privilege of leading my own company. My journey is proof that you, too, can build a thriving and rewarding career in this field, whatever success looks like for you. Whether that's earning a six-figure salary, leading diverse teams, contributing to groundbreaking studies, or building your own clinical research business, your goals are valid and within reach.

I am always reminded that beyond the titles and the financial milestones, let's not forget the heart of what we do. Clinical research is about people. Every data point represents a person. This is someone who volunteered, often in the face of uncertainty, to advance science and help future patients. I want to take a moment to acknowledge and thank the trial participants whose courage and generosity make our work possible. Without them, there would be no progress, no cures, and no innovations. As you move forward in your career, may you always honor their contribution through your commitment to ethical, high-quality research. These are the unsung heroes.

Working in clinical research is very rewarding. There's a unique satisfaction in knowing that your efforts, whether coordinating a study visit, managing data, monitoring a site, or leading a team, all play a direct role in bringing new treatments to the world. It's a field where you not only grow professionally but also leave a lasting impact on public health and patient care. Every step you take in mastering this craft brings you closer to making a difference on a global scale.

So, as you close this chapter and begin the next phase of your journey, remember that you are capable of achieving great things in clinical research. Stay committed to learning, stay open to opportunities, and stay connected to the purpose that brought you here. I believe in your potential to rise, to lead, and to build a career that is not only successful but also meaningful. Your pathway to mastery and fulfillment starts now. I can't wait to see where it takes you.

As you embark on your journey to mastering clinical research, please remember you don't have to do it alone. I invite you to stay connected with a community of professionals who, like you, are committed to advancing their careers and making a difference in the field. Join me at SpringWell360, where we provide ongoing support, resources, and mentorship for aspiring and seasoned clinical research professionals alike.

Are you looking to sharpen your skills even further? Explore my courses and workshops designed to help you navigate every stage of your career, from landing your first role, to GCPs, or preparing for an audit, to stepping into leadership positions, and even building your own business in clinical research. Let's continue this journey together. Stay inspired, stay informed, and stay committed to your growth and success.

Visit www.SpringWell360.com to access tools, join the community, and get exclusive updates. Your next step toward a six-figure, purpose-driven career in clinical research starts today. And I'll be right here cheering you on every step of the way. Here is to your success, your growth, and your impact.

References

These sources were used to guide the content of this book.

Blackstock, U. (2024). *Legacy: A Black physician reckons with racism in medicine*. Penguin.

Bowers, D. (2008). *Medical statistics from scratch: An introduction for health professionals (2nd ed.)*. John Wiley & Sons.

D'Agostino, R. B., Sullivan, L. M., & Beiser, A. S. (2006). *Introductory applied biostatistics*. Brooks Cole.

Gray, F. D. (2013). *The Tuskegee syphilis study: The real story and beyond*. NewSouth Books.

Hulley, S. B., Cummings, S. R., Browner, W. S., Grady, D. G., & Newman, T. B. (2007). *Designing clinical research (3rd ed.)*. Lippincott Williams & Wilkins.

McFadden, E. (2007). *Management of data in clinical trials (2nd ed.)*. John Wiley & Sons.

Ng, R. (2009). *Drugs: From discovery to approval (2nd ed.)*. Wiley-Blackwell.

Skloot, R. (2019). *The immortal life of Henrietta Lacks*. Pan Macmillan.

Spilker, B. (2009). *Guide to drug development: A comprehensive review and assessment*. Lippincott Williams & Wilkins.

Washington, H. A. (2008). *Medical apartheid: The dark history of medical experimentation on Black Americans from colonial times to the present*. Vintage.

About the Author

Dr. Nadine Spring public health professional, clinical research expert, and educator dedicated to advancing health equity and increasing diversity in clinical trials. She is the founder of SpringWell360, she provides education and consulting services on clinical research, recruitment strategies, and ethical considerations in health equity. Through her YouTube channel, online courses, and workshops, she empowers aspiring professionals with the tools to excel in public health and clinical research. She is also an Assistant Professor and Associate Director of the Public Health program at the University of Bridgeport, where she teaches, mentors students and guides them through their integrated learning experiences.

With a background in clinical research operations, Dr. Spring has worked with research firms and academic institutions to improve patient recruitment strategies and community health outreach. Her expertise stems from her research on increasing the participation of women of color in clinical trials, a topic she has presented at conferences and expert panels.

LinkedIn: https://www.linkedin.com/in/nadinespring/
Facebook: https://www.facebook.com/people/SpringWell360-LLC/100087145188043/
Instagram: https://www.instagram.com/springwell360/
Website: www.springwell360.com

📣 Your Next Step Starts Now

You've just finished reading *Mastering Clinical Research*—and that means you're already ahead of the curve.

But don't stop here.

Imagine what's possible when you have **ongoing guidance, community support, and next-level tools** to turn everything you've learned into a real-world six-figure career.

✅ Ready to refine your resume and land your first or next clinical role?

✅ Want exclusive templates, interview prep, and real-time job strategy tips?

✅ Looking for mentorship and a network of like-minded professionals?

👉 **Here's what to do next:**

Join our Course Clinical Trials 360

🎯 **Visit www.springwell360.com**

You'll get access to:

- Bonus tools and downloadable templates
- Tips for advancing your career
- Opportunities to book 1:1 strategy sessions with me
- And priority access to new trainings and career-building programs

Don't wait—your six-figure pathway is already in motion. Let's keep building it **together**.

Click the link below to take the next step.
The future you've been working toward is just one click away.

www.springwell360.com

Thank you for trusting me to be part of your journey.
I can't wait to see where you go next.

www.ingramcontent.com/pod-product-compliance
Lightning Source LLC
Chambersburg PA
CBHW071330120626
46546CB00002B/512